SMALL MIRACLE

SMALL MIRACLE

A Play in Three Acts

BY

NORMAN KRASNA

WITH A PREFACE BY
GEORGE ABBOTT

SAMUEL FRENCH

NEW YORK   LOS ANGELES
SAMUEL FRENCH Ltd.   LONDON
1935

MANUFACTURED IN THE UNITED STATES OF AMERICA
BY THE VAIL-BALLOU PRESS, INC., BINGHAMTON, N. Y.

FOR

MY MOTHER,

BEATRICE MANNISON KRASNA

PREFACE

I will now constitute myself a critic. I find it a pleasant change, and not a particularly difficult one. It is much easier to criticize a play than to write one, a fact which a few of "the boys" who have made an attempt at playwrighting have found out.

This is a good play. Its virtues far outnumber its faults. Many a good play makes tedious reading, but I think that "Small Miracle" is exciting in either form. It is modern. It offers no superfluous information. It disregards the old rule that we used to learn in Professor Baker's course that all facts should be told three times. It is reticent and yet lucid. And it glows with feeling and insight, especially in the scene between Tony and Taft at the opening of Act II.

Its greatest virtue is not visible on the surface—its technique. Here is a play with half a dozen themes so skillfully interwoven that each blends and has its effect upon the other. And herein, also, lies its greatest flaw— it is at times implausible—it is at times almost as implausible as life. The possibility of these interlocking incidents actually taking place as they do may bother the realist. The skill with which it is done so stimulates me, that I forgive all.

Mr. Krasna has gathered into the lounge room of his theatre a wide assortment of people, all of whom are real. Many of them you will recognize. They are already among your acquaintances. And although some of the others may not be people whom you desire for neighbors, yet I know that, at a safe distance, you will find them interesting. His people are truer than his play: and both are exciting, which, I fancy, is one of the things that really all good creative work should be.

GEORGE ABBOTT

"SMALL MIRACLE" was first produced by Courtney Burr at the Golden Theatre in New York City on September 26, 1934. The play was staged by George Abbott, the setting was designed by Boris Aronson, and the cast was as follows:

CARL BARRETT, JR.	Played by	*Edward Crandall*
TONY MAKO	" "	*Joseph Spurin-Calleia*
JOSEPH TAFT	" "	*Joseph King*
MA	" "	*Eva Condon*
HERMAN	" "	*William Wadsworth*
WILLIAM S. JOHNSON	" "	*G. Albert Smith*
EDDIE	" "	*Myron McCormick*
MAE DANISH	" "	*Elspeth Eric*
MAC MASON	" "	*Wyrley Birch*
HELEN	" "	*Fraye Gilbert*
REPAIR MAN	" "	*James Lane*
SYLVIA TEMPLE	" "	*Ilka Chase*
ANNA	" "	*Lucille Strudwick*
KITTY	" "	*Jean Bellows*
TWELVE-YEAR-OLD GIRL	" "	*Edna Hagan*
STANLEY MADISON	" "	*George Lambert*
MRS. MADISON	" "	*Violet Barney*
DONALD MADISON	" "	*Hitous Gray*
FRANK	" "	*Juan Varro*
GEORGE NELSON	" "	*Allan Hale*
CAPTAIN SEAVER	" "	*Robert Middlemass*
HEALY	" "	*Herbert Duffy*
ANDERSON	" "	*Owen Martin*
FIRST GIRL	" "	*Helen Gardner*
SECOND GIRL	" "	*Nancy Vane*

And Others

The scene is the Lounge of the 43rd St. Theatre.

Act I

A few moments before the rise of the curtain on the play occupying the 43rd St. Theatre.

Act II

Concurrent with the Second Act of the play in the 43rd St. Theatre.

Act III

Concurrent with the Third Act of the play in the 43rd St. Theatre.

Note: The music heard off stage does not purport to be any single, recognizable score; merely arbitrary selections of various composers.

ACT ONE

ACT ONE

*Up goes the curtain, and we are in the lounge
of one of the newer theatres; paneled in dark
wood; furnished with upholstered couches
and easy chairs; thickly carpeted; indirectly
lighted; a pleasant, inviting room for theatre-
goers to congregate and smoke between acts.
Happily, the dimensions of such a lounge just
fit our stage. The stairway, Right, faces our
audience. Another staircase, Left, exposes a
few steps and twists out of sight. Two doors,
the entrances to the Ladies' and Gentlemen's
rooms, are three-quarters, respectively, Right
and Left. The doors are knobless and swing
in, and are almost entirely concealed by two-
piece velvet drapes suspended curtain-fashion.
Comfortable couches Right and Left, a few
easy chairs, and a low table not quite Back
Centre compose the furniture, arranged in
usual semi-circle fashion to leave a clearing for
smokers and chatterers. A built-in drinking
fountain is Centre, a waste-basket beneath it.
Rear, prominent, is a telephone booth built-in.
It is lighted. Extreme Left, down stage, is a
dial slot telephone. Two adjacent swinging
panels, Right, under the staircase, are* EDDIE'S
and MAC'S *lockers.*

The play occupying the theatre is a musical comedy, and during the progression of our play we hear the musical numbers. From time to time we hear laughter and applause.

As The Curtain Rises: A few persons are already peopling our lounge room.

WILLIAM JOHNSON *enters from staircase Right. He is twenty-five, probably an excellent bank teller, slightly unkempt in his present crisis. He looks at the dial phone, looks to see if there is another, spies the phone booth and crosses to it. Enters the phone booth. We see him through the glass, and from his pantomime and murmur we realize the call is important to* MR. JOHNSON. *At a crescendo in the unintelligible dialogue from the booth,* CARL *looks up once and goes back to his cross word puzzle.*

Our Characters On Are: CARL BARRETT, JR., *of the original Philadelphia Barretts, polished to glinting, whose English tailored full dress proves a gentleman. He is thirty years of age, but a young thirty years what with a roundish face, a life-long non-indulgence in work, and a tennis court slimness. He has never been serious or hurt in his life, and won't be in this play. He lounges on the couch, Centre, reading a newspaper.*

TONY MAKO *sits on the couch, Left. He is stocky and swarthy, with a milder face than his trade needs. He might be twenty-eight, and his Italian accent is faint because it has been*

*acquired on the East Side. He wears a tight
blue pin-stripe suit and patent leather shoes.
He smokes.*

JOSEPH TAFT *sits with* MAKO. *He is forty
years of age, slighty grey, bulky, with an intelligent, broad face. A topcoat is slung over
his arm, nearest* MAKO. *A cigar stub is in his
mouth.*

*As we said, the Curtain is up. And on this
tableau we remain for fifteen seconds.* CARL
BARRETT, JR., *then folds his paper into a
square, the better to work the cross word puzzle, extracts a gold pencil from his inside
pocket, and commences to fill it in. From the
staircase, Left, an elderly couple enter. We
shall know them only as* MA *and* HERMAN.

*This visit to a legitimate theatre is an adven-
ture, and while they seem brave enough on
their entrance we know they are not. They advance to the Centre of the stage, both looking
for directions, and spy the signs.*

HERMAN. [*Quietly, in the presence of strangers.*] I'll
meet you here. [MA *enters one door,* HERMAN *the
other.*]

MAKO. [*Depositing his cigarette stub in a floor tray.*]
Maybe the show already started?

JOE. We'll know when it starts.

MAKO. You think we got time for another cigarette?

JOE. Yeah, sure. [*A* TWELVE YEAR OLD GIRL *runs from
Right and into Ladies' room.*]

MAKO. I smoke about four packs of these a day.

JOE. That's a lot, it might not be good for you.

MAKO. [*Looking grimly at* JOE, *after a pause.*] It might not be good for me! You think I ought to take care of my health, eh, for my old age? [JOHNSON *has exited from the phone booth and seated himself on the couch, Right.* CARL *has taken a cigarette from his case and is searching in his pocket for a match.* JOHNSON *sees this and strikes a match for* CARL.]

JOHNSON. Match?

CARL. Thanks.

JOHNSON. [*Dying to get it off his chest.*] I'm getting in practice. I expect to be handing out cigars pretty soon.

CARL. Is that so?

JOHNSON. [*Expansively.*] I'll be a father any time now. My wife's in the hospital having a baby, right this minute.

CARL. Congratulations. I hope everything turns out all right.

JOHNSON. [*Now he's nervous.*] I hope so too. I've been reading where four and a half out of every hundred mothers aren't constituted to have babies.

CARL. [*Just a statement.*] Four and a half.

JOHNSON. And the trouble is you don't know whether you're one of the four and a half until you find out.

CARL. [*To get back to the cross word puzzle.*] Well, don't worry. You've got the percentage in your favor.

JOHNSON. [*Too airily.*] Oh, I'm not worrying.

[BARRETT *is looking at his paper.* JOHNSON *is standing glumly, worrying, and* MA *enters from Ladies'. She does not see* HERMAN. *Buzz-buzz, the electric buzzer signifying the curtain.* CARL *puts his paper down, and his pencil in his pocket.* JOHNSON *starts Right. From the head of the stairs, barely visible,* EDDIE *announces:*]

EDDIE. Curtain going up. Curtain! [*He disappears quickly, back to his coat room.*]

JOE. Ready?

MAKO. No—not yet. [MA, *who has appeared, looks anxiously toward the door for* HERMAN. CARL *and* JOHNSON *are exiting Right.* MAKO, *relaxing, lets his head fall back on the couch.* JOE *looks at him.* HERMAN *exits from Men's and* MA *sees him.*]

HERMAN. [*Both walking up the stairs, Right.*] Say, some bathroom!

MA. You ought to see Roxy's! [*They are off.*]

JOE. [*Noticing that* MAKO *has now leaned forward, his hand over his eyes, his elbow on his knee.*] What's the matter—you sick? [MAKO *is too ill to answer, he rubs his face in his palm.*] Take it easy, Tony. [*They both rise and start to the Men's room. Just as they reach it,* JOE *removes the topcoat which has been over his right arm and* MAKO'S *left. As* MAKO *enters the room first, we see he is handcuffed to* JOE. *Our* TWELVE YEAR OLD GIRL *runs from the Ladies' room to the drinking fountain and up Right staircase. From above, the overture starts.*]

FIRST GIRL. [*Coming out of Ladies' room and going*

hurriedly Right.] It might be just a coincidence, but the last three nights I went out with him I had to pay for the cab.

SECOND GIRL. All I can tell you is, he showed up for a week-end with no clothes but the ones he had on his back. [*They are off.* JOE *and* MAKO *enter from Men's room.*]

JOE. Feel better?

MAKO. [*Flatly.*] I'm all right.

JOE. [*Starting.*] Let's go up. [*They walk across the stage, Right, and then* JOE *halts.*] Wait a minute. I'm not going to enjoy this show. I better call up the office. [*He walks to the phone booth and enters,* JOE *leaning against the door, looking up in the direction of the music. He dials.*] Let me talk to Captain Seaver . . . Seaver, this is Joe. . . . I missed the train. . . . I just missed it by two minutes. . . . Well, the next train is one o'clock in the morning and I got over four hours to kill. Well, I was going to take him back to the Tombs but you know Boy-Scout Benson! He'd report it to the commissioner just for the hell of it! . . . Yeah, it's only four hours. . . . Yeah. . . . You want us to go where? . . . to a movie? . . . You want to hear something funny? I'm calling you from the Forty-Third Street Theatre right now. . . . No. . . . It's a musical show. So are you. O.K. Seaver. . . . So long. [*He hangs up and they both start Right, passing* EDDIE *who enters.* EDDIE *is the coat-room boy, twenty-two, intelligent looking, attired in an appropriate uniform. He looks the room over. On the carpet, where* CARL *sat, is the first cigarette he threw on the floor.* EDDIE *goes over*

*and picks it up. He takes the newspaper from the couch
and goes to throw both the cigarette butt and the paper
into the waste-basket under the slot machine.*] That's off
my mind. They raise hell downtown if you don't report
every little thing. The only detective work they do down
there is find out our mistakes and run to the commissioner with them. [*They are off. Before they are out of
sight,* MAE *is coming down the steps, Left.* JOE *and*
MAKO *have just missed seeing her.* EDDIE *looks back at
them to see that they are out of earshot.* MAE, *who has
come directly to him, looks at their retreating backs until
they are gone.* MAE *is* EDDIE'S *age, blonde, a trifle hard,
and the theatre's senior usher, also in uniform.*]

EDDIE. [*Anxiously.*] What'd he say?

MAE. Aren't you going to kiss me? [EDDIE, *just slightly
reluctant leans forward. Evidently* MAE *expected a more
fervent embrace, for she starts to put her arms around
him, but* EDDIE *has drawn back already.*]

EDDIE. What'd he say, Mae?

MAE. Don't worry, Eddie. Please, it's beginning to show
on you.

EDDIE. I'm all right. Mae, did you go to that doctor?

MAE. I just came from there.

[*Our Overture dies out.*]

EDDIE. Well? [*She says nothing.*] Is it all right?

MAE. You mean will he do it?

EDDIE. Yes.

MAE. [*Hesitantly.*] He told me to come Friday.

EDDIE. Friday? Don't be frightened, Mae. It's nothing. Lots of women do it and nothing ever happens.

MAE. I'm not afraid, Eddie. I don't know what I'd do though if it wasn't for you.

EDDIE. Everything'll be all right. He understood about the money? How I'd pay him? [MAE's *face falls.* EDDIE *is nervous.*] What's the matter? Didn't you tell him? [*Another pause from* MAE.] You told him, didn't you?

MAE. He wouldn't do it.

EDDIE. He wouldn't?

MAE. I begged him but he said he never broke his rule. [*She looks at him too carefully.*] I told him I'd pay him Friday.

EDDIE. Friday? The whole two hundred dollars?

MAE. Yes.

EDDIE. Where are we going to get it? What'd you tell him that for?

MAE. Don't be angry, Eddie, I had to. He wouldn't trust me. He said what he's doing is illegal and if somebody doesn't want to pay him he can't do anything about it.

EDDIE. But didn't you tell him what I told you? That I got a steady job and I'll pay him something every week? I'll sign a regular promissory note?

MAE. Yes.

EDDIE. Well, what'd he say?

MAE. He wouldn't do it. [*She looks squarely at him.*] I don't understand you, Eddie. I don't even know if you want to help me. You got the money.

EDDIE. Mae, you know what that money is for.

MAE. Well, what's more important? Your law school or what I'm up against?

EDDIE. It isn't that. Won't you try and understand? I can be finished with law school in June. It's taken me all year to save up that hundred and fifty dollars and in school if you haven't got it they suspend you. Can't you see what that means to me? I've been working like this since I've been sixteen—and now that I'm almost out you're asking me to lose a whole year.

MAE. [*Pitifully.*] What do you want me to do?

EDDIE. Give me the address of that doctor. I'll go to him tomorrow and talk to him. You'll see, he'll trust me—

MAE. [*For some reason she now bursts into tears, crying into her hands.*] You don't want to help me.

EDDIE. [*Giving up his pleading entirely. In a desperate voice.*] Oh, stop crying! I'll give you the money! I'll give you a hundred and sixty dollars—he'll take that for a down payment!

MAE. You think I'm unreasonable. You don't know how a girl feels.

EDDIE. All right, I'll give you the money tomorrow.

MAE. Maybe by Friday you can think of somebody to borrow it from.

EDDIE. [*Bitterly.*] I've thought of everybody. You know who I asked yesterday?

MAE. Who?

EDDIE. Helen!

MAE. Helen! Did you tell her about me?

EDDIE. And I should have told her sooner.

MAE. What did she say to you?

EDDIE. [*Evenly, pointedly.*] She loves me. What do you think she said? [MAE *would answer, but she sees* MAC *entering Right.* MAC MASON *is fifty-five, grey, part bald, a kindly, inoffensive, oddly religious soul. He is the ticket-taker of the theatre, and sees that the established routine is maintained. He wears a dinner coat and derby.*]

MAE. I'll see you later. [*She passes* MAC, *exiting Right.*]

MAC. [*Who is crossing to his locker, Right—looks after her.*] What's the matter with Mae?

EDDIE. Nothing. She's all right.

MAC. [*Opening the panel locker with his finger-nails.*] You better hang around the balcony, Eddie, there's an intoxicated feller up there.

EDDIE. All right. [*But he stays, thinking.*]

MAC. Don't offer to give him his money back. Just ask him to keep quiet.

EDDIE. Mac—I want to ask you a favor. It's a pretty big favor.

MAC. Why, certainly, my boy, what is it?

EDDIE. You've known me a long time, Mac; you know I'm not dishonest.

MAC. Of course you're not, who said you were?

EDDIE. [*Hard to get to the point.*] Nobody.

MAC. Is it a reference you want? I'll give you the best reference there is.

EDDIE. No.

MAC. You're a good boy, Eddie. You're a fine boy. I wish you were my son.

EDDIE. Thanks.

MAC. [*Reminding himself.*] Eddie, I just remembered —I want to ask you something. If you can't do it now don't be ashamed to say so. Just say it.

EDDIE. [*Fearfully.*] What is it?

MAC. The rent's sort of caught me sudden. If you can spare thirty dollars for about two weeks— [*He sees the reaction on* EDDIE's *face.*] Eddie—it's all right. Don't feel bad about it, I know you got your own expenses. I'll manage fine. [*He turns back to probing in his locker. He takes a revolver out which he puts in his coat pocket.*]

EDDIE. Mac, that was the favor I was going to ask you. Only I was going to ask for two hundred dollars.

MAC. Two hundred dollars! [*He comes toward* EDDIE.] Lad, why do you need that much money?

EDDIE. Oh, I need it. [*He looks up, not to worry* MAC.] For school. It takes a lot of money to get to be a lawyer.

MAC. Have courage, Eddie. You know what the Book says—as ye sow so also shall ye reap. I never went to college—and look what I am now—a ticket-taker. [MAC *has taken the gun out of his coat pocket to transfer to his trouser pocket, but has gestured with it in* EDDIE's *direction.*]

EDDIE. Mac! Be careful! [MAC *holds it aside.*] Why do you carry that, it'll only go off some day?

MAC. [*Looking at it.*] I'm deathly afraid of it, but I have to carry it. The insurance man was around tonight. He said if anybody tries to hold up the box-office I have to shoot them. [*He puts it in his back pocket.*]

EDDIE. I can just see you doing it.

MAC. [*Shaking his head.*] It is not for Man to take his brother's life. Life belongs to God. He giveth all. He taketh all. Even a mosquito on my hand—I wouldn't kill it.

EDDIE. [*Pleasantly.*] What do you do, just leave it there?

MAC. I'd frighten it away.

EDDIE. I don't know, Mac. Someday a mosquito'll drop dead of fright.

MAC. [*Smiles, tolerant.*] Eddie, you're not religious. That's because you're young. I used to be like that, never believed in anything. But I know now—there's not a bird in the sky, there's not a fish in the sea—that God in His Almighty wisdom does not look out for. I know it.

EDDIE. Well, I believe in God.

MAC. [*Practically from a pulpit.*] But do you believe in God's miracles? Do you believe He can do the Impossible? The miraculous? Turn wrong into right—lie into truth—sin into purity—with a flick of His little finger? [*And he flicks, like God.*]

EDDIE. That's a little old-fashioned, Mac. Nobody be-

lieves in that kind of religion any more, that God goes
around helping people by miracles. Did you ever hear
of a miracle?

MAC. God opened the Red Sea for the Hebrews, and
saved them from the Egyptians.

EDDIE. That was a little before our time, Mac. What religion needs nowadays is another miracle. If the Hudson
River ever opened in half, for instance, that'd be something. Church'd be so crowded they'd have to play two
performances a day.

MAC. There are miracles today, there are. There may not
be big miracles, but there may be small miracles. An
automobile passing in the street—a rainstorm from
heaven—maybe even an accident—who knows; some
little thing— [*And just then the telephone in the booth
rings. It is not the ordinary recurring ring, but one con-
tinuous peal.* MAC *and* EDDIE *look toward the booth.*]

EDDIE. Mac—a miracle!

MAC. Who knows—it might be. [*Going to the booth.*]
That's a very peculiar ringing. [*As he goes to the
phone,* EDDIE *exits Left.*] Hello. . . . Hello. . . .
Hello! [*He puts the receiver back on the hook. As he
steps out of the booth he talks, not knowing* EDDIE *has
gone.*] That's funny, it's dead. [*Applause and laughter
until* MAC *goes to the other phone, taking a nickel out of
his vest pocket, which he puts into the slot. He rings
operator.*] Operator? My telephone is out of order. All
right, give it to me. [*The nickel is returned. He dials
114.*] Repair Service? One of our telephones is dead.
It just rang and then when I answered it there wasn't

any buzzing. . . . Can't somebody come around to-night? This telephone has to be used. . . . It's the telephone in the lounge room of the Forty-Third Street Theatre . . . [*In a surprised voice.*] On Forty-third Street, where did you think? Why don't you look in the telephone book? You're welcome. [*He is chuckling at his sally. He turns and sees* HELEN *coming down the staircase, Right.* HELEN *is dark, with small features, big eyes, and an appealing personality. She wears street clothes, a coat and hat. Her entrance is hesitant.*]

HELEN. Are you Mister Mason?

MAC. Yes ma'm.

HELEN. The man in the box-office said I could ask you if you'd let me speak to one of the ushers—it'll only be a minute.

MAC. [*Still cheerily.*] Well, I think that can be arranged. Who do you want to speak to?

HELEN. Miss Danish. Thank you very much. It's really important and I'll only be a minute.

MAC. [*Starting upstairs Left.*] No trouble at all, she'll be right down. [*He goes off.* HELEN *looks around, goes to centre couch and sits. She sits for a few seconds, her nervousness being apparent. From Left comes* MAE.]

MAE. [*From the steps.*] Are you looking for me?

HELEN. [*Turns quickly, looks for a second.*] Are you Mae?

MAE. [*Guardedly.*] Yes.

HELEN. I'm Helen. I guess Eddie's told you about me.

MAE. He mentioned something.

HELEN. We're engaged to be married.

MAE. No, he never mentioned that. [*Walks to couch.*] I'm sort of engaged to him myself.

HELEN. He told me about it last night. That's what I want to talk to you about. [MAE, *who in the dueling is much more possessed, seats herself. From a breast pocket she takes a cigarette, which she lights and smokes during the scene.*]

MAE. [*She holds the package out.*] Cigarette?

HELEN. [*Not even noticing the cigarettes.*] You've got to let him out of this trouble.

MAE. Let *him* out? Say, what'd he tell you?

HELEN. He told me everything. And that you want two hundred dollars. If you knew what that money means to him—and how he scraped it together—working, day and night—even going without food sometimes—you couldn't touch a penny of it.

MAE. [*Evenly, too quietly.*] What do you think that money means to me?

HELEN. [*For a second she looks into her gloves.*] I realize that. I know you need the money. [*Pleading.*] But isn't there anybody you can borrow it from? We'll both pay it back, we'll give you something every week.

MAE. No, I don't know anybody in this town. I'm all alone.

HELEN. [*After chewing her underlip, determinedly.*] You're not going to ruin his whole life. He's going to be a lawyer! It'd be different if this was a love affair, but it wasn't—you knew what you were doing!

MAE. And I know what I'm doing right now. He doesn't have to give me the money. He can marry me.

HELEN. He doesn't want to marry you!

MAE. I don't know if he wants to—but I know he has to.

HELEN. I won't let him marry you! I'll marry him first!

MAE. Oh no you won't! There's a law about that— [EDDIE *has come down the steps, Right, on the preceding speech.*]

EDDIE. [*From the steps.*] Helen! [*He comes down quickly.*] Why'd you come here? [*He has gone to* HELEN, *both* GIRLS *are silent.*] Please go, Helen, I'll straighten this out myself.

MAE. [*Getting up.*] I don't see what's to be straightened out. I'm being made to look unreasonable. God knows I'm not asking for any picnic for myself. If you're not going to give me that two hundred dollars you'll marry me. And tomorrow!

EDDIE. Marry you?

HELEN. He never will!

MAE. Say, what right have you got to be angry? Do you think I want to marry you! What am I asking for —a favor? I'm sorry I ever laid my eyes on you! And I hope two minutes after I marry you, you drop dead!

[*She exits Left.* HELEN *stands for a second, and then slips on to the couch, crying into her hands.* EDDIE *is miserable.*]

EDDIE. Helen, there's no use crying.

HELEN. [*Sobbing.*] How could you have had anything to do with her?

EDDIE. [*Futilely.*] Everything'll come out all right.

HELEN. [*Wiping her eyes with her handkerchief.*] We're going to get married—tomorrow morning. [EDDIE *runs his hand through his hair.*] What can she do to you, legally, if we get married?

EDDIE. I don't know. Nothing I guess—she's over twenty-one—except sue me for money. The only thing is next year—when I come up for admission to the Bar—

HELEN. Couldn't it be explained? Couldn't you go to them now—before she did anything—

EDDIE. No. Not a morals charge. I know someone who got arrested for drunken driving on New Year's Eve— three years ago—and they didn't let him in.

HELEN. We'll have to get the money. We'll just have to. Have you asked *everybody* you know? Maybe they'll each lend you a little?

EDDIE. I asked everybody. I sent wires to relatives I've never seen. They don't even answer. [*From Left,* MAC *and the telephone* REPAIR MAN *come down. The* REPAIR MAN *is dressed in an ordinary business suit, wears a hat, and carries a small bag, containing tools, wire, cards, etc.*]

MAC. Eddie, there's a lady been waiting to check a fur coat for five minutes. She's calling for you.

EDDIE. [*Hurriedly.*] Helen, go up to the balcony and see the show. We'll go home together.

HELEN. [*Dead.*] I told him I'd go right out.

MAC. [*Indicating booth phone.*] That's the one.

EDDIE. Mac, this is my girl. She can sit in the balcony, can't she?

MAC. [*Tipping his hat.*] Why certainly, miss.

EDDIE. Don't worry, darling. Please. [*He squeezes her arm and runs, Right, two steps at a time.* HELEN *sits, sick. After a few seconds she will get up and exit, Right.*]

MAC. There isn't any charge for this, is there?

REPAIR MAN. No. Was anybody using the phone when it got out of order?

MAC. No. I was standing here— [*He points.*] and it began to ring, by itself, which was pretty funny, because nobody calls here—they always call the box office. In fact, I thought it was a wrong number, but when I went to answer it—it was just dead—no buzzing like you always hear, or anything.

REPAIR MAN. [*Pulls the light cord to extinguish it.*] Well, it isn't a local trouble. I'll have to check from the office.

MAC. There was something odd about the ringing. I remember remarking about it. It rang steady right until I took the receiver off.

REPAIR MAN. Well, I'm not sure what it is exactly. [*He tacks an "Out of Order" sign on door.*] We get a dead phone for a lot of reasons—a cable sets itself, or water soaks in—or a short circuit some place—it could be anything.

MAC. Isn't the company going to fix it?

REPAIR MAN. Why, certainly. We'll trace it down in no time. It might even start to work again by itself—that happens.

MAC. You're sure no one's going to get an electricity shock, and sue the theatre?

REPAIR MAN. No. If it's a short circuit and it corrects itself, it might ring again. If it does, and you're here, just count ten before you take the receiver off; it'll be working. Just count ten.

MAC. I hope it fixes itself tonight—we use that phone a lot.

REPAIR MAN. It isn't so bad—you've still got the other phone.

MAC. But we need them both. We could use three phones during intermission. And a lot of people want to talk private.

REPAIR MAN. [*Gathering up his bag.*] It'll be all right in a couple of hours. [*They both exit—Left—talking.*]

MAC. Do you want me to make a report on this?

REPAIR MAN. You don't have to. A dead phone for a couple hours never hurt anybody.

MAC. [*Chuckling.*] I guess not.

REPAIR MAN. This happens once in a million times. [*They are off.* KITTY, *an usher, has come from Left and gone to the coffee table, busying herself with the cups.* CARL *enters, Right, and walks slowly down the steps. Halfway down he turns and spies* SYLVIA *descending the staircase on the opposite side of the stage. She is not yet visible to the audience. He stops and looks at her without changing his expression. Both of them now continue.* CARL *goes to the centre couch and sits,* SYLVIA *to the water fountain, taking a cup and drinking.* KITTY *exits Left.* SYLVIA *looks at the back of* CARL'S *head and talks easily.*]

SYLVIA. I saw you from the back of the theatre, and I kept calling at the top of my voice for the coat boy so you'd hear me.

CARL. [*Not even turning around.*] I heard you, dear, clear as a bell. [SYLVIA *comes over to him. She looks toward the Right and then kisses him.*]

SYLVIA. [*Low.*] Still?

CARL. What do you think?

SYLVIA. More than Wednesday?

CARL. Uh huh.

SYLVIA. More than last Friday?

CARL. [*Not seriously.*] Last Friday? I didn't see you last Friday! You've been cheating!

SYLVIA. [*Not at all frightened.*] It was last Friday. [*Evenly.*] I remember every time. [CARL *leans over and kisses her lightly. Then he reaches into his vest*

pocket and extracts a key, which he holds up. SYLVIA
looks at him and takes it, smiling.]

CARL. Do you think you'll remember the apartment?

SYLVIA. I might.

CARL. What floor is it on?

SYLVIA. The third.

CARL. [*In burlesque excitement.*] See that! It's the
fourth!

SYLVIA. Is it? I have another lover on the third floor,
it confuses me.

CARL. You go over to my place and I'll follow you in
about fifteen minutes.

SYLVIA. Darling, something's happened. I thought
Tippy was going to use the car and chauffeur—he always does—and I'd come here in a cab.

CARL. But he didn't!

SYLVIA. So's not to look suspicious—I had to keep the
chauffeur.

CARL. Why didn't you dismiss him?

SYLVIA. Darling, how could I be sure you were going
to be here, after that beautiful evening I spent at the
National Geographic Museum. I'll tell you what. We
can sneak out now, and be back here by the end of the
show.

CARL. Oh!—Oh! I wouldn't trust that driver of yours
around the corner. He looks to me like one of those
conscientious employees you always read about in divorce actions. On the aforementioned date I followed

the aforesaid lady to the aforementioned apartment. [*Shaking his head.*] No, dear. I'm afraid we'll have to sit this one out. [*He puts his hand out.*] Give me the key.

SYLVIA. [*Drawing her fist to her.*] No.

CARL. [*Still holding his hand out.*] Come, come, Sylvia. [SYLVIA *gives it to him abruptly, her pride suddenly hurt that she has been begging. She walks to couch Left, and sits.*] Now, darling, let's be grown-up. I'm only doing this for you. Your recklessness is very flattering, but we're not taking any chauffeurs into our confidence.

SYLVIA. All right.

CARL. [*Going to her.*] Just staying here together for the whole show is dangerous. We might meet someone we know—and they'd ask who you were with and who I was with—and then someone'd notice the lovelight in my eyes— [*She softens now and smiles at him.*]— other people are just as clever as we are—

SYLVIA. [*Patting his hand.*] They're not as clever as you, darling.

CARL. Now the best defense is a good offense. [*He reaches for a coin.*] Go to the phone, call up our mutual friend, your husband, tell him not to work too hard— and that you've bumped into me—casual-like. [*She takes the coin.*] Then all rumors that reach his shell pink ears will be discounted.

SYLVIA. [*She goes to the phone booth.*] Do you think he's at the office?

CARL. I know he is, I had dinner with him, personally; then I took him back to the office, personally—and then I came right here. [JOHNSON *appears, Right.*]

SYLVIA. Impersonally. [*She sees the sign.*] It's out of order.

CARL. There's another. [JOHNSON *has come from the staircase, Right, and in crossing to the dial phone is in* SYLVIA'S *path. They both stop at the same time.*]

SYLVIA. [*Pleasantly.*] It's all right. I'm in no hurry.

JOHNSON. Excuse me. [*He puts a coin in the slot and dials.*] The fourth floor, please. [*To* SYLVIA, *apologetically.*] I'm a little anxious about this call. You see, I'm having a baby—with my wife— [*Someone has spoken in his ear.*] Hello? Fourth floor? Is Samuel Neil there? Mister Neil? Can I speak to him, please? [*To Sylvia.*] It's our first baby. [*Back in phone.*] Hello, Sam! What's happened? Oh, oh! But everything's all right so far, isn't it? You're not holding anything back, are you? Yeah, I'm still at the theatre. How's Ruth? It's a great play—you're sure everything's all right? Yeah, O.K. [*He gestures to hang up, and then reminds himself.*] Sam! They can't tell whether— [*Evidently* SAM *has hung up. He does, too, and starts for stairs, Left.*]

SYLVIA. I hope everything's all right.

JOHNSON. [*Distractedly.*] Yes, sure, everything's fine. Only I feel like I ought to be at the hospital. You see, I didn't want to come to the show tonight, but they made me. [*He addresses them both.*] You know, it's a funny thing. I don't see how they had babies a hundred years ago—with no hospitals, and no ether—and no doctors—

CARL. And no telephones.

JOHNSON. Yeah. It's a wonder we're here now.

SYLVIA. They had a hard time in those days.

JOHNSON. I guess so. Our family's got a great story about being born. My grandmother used to tell it to me all the time. You know what it is?

SYLVIA. [*Amused.*] No, what is it?

JOHNSON. Well, her father—my grandmother's father —was born in a taxicab!

SYLVIA. In a taxicab!

JOHNSON. What do you think of that?

CARL. You mean your great-grandfather?

JOHNSON. Yep.

CARL. There weren't any taxicabs in those days. [JOHNSON *is blank-faced.* SYLVIA *looks from one to the other.*]

JOHNSON. [*Thinking furiously.*] Say, that's right. There couldn't have been.

SYLVIA. [*Jumping in.*] She probably meant a carriage. They had carriages.

JOHNSON. [*Shaking his head—slowly.*] No—she said in a taxicab. I can just hear her saying it. "Me fayther was borrn in a taxi-cabb." She had an accent—Irish. [*He thinks again.*] Nobody in the whole family ever thought of that. [*He turns, to exit Left—flatly.*] Ha!

That's some joke! [*He exits.* SYLVIA *and* CARL *watch him go.*]

CARL. Very bright family that.

SYLVIA. [*Going to phone and putting in nickel, and dialing.*] You've probably spoiled the only thing the family had to boast about.

CARL. Do you know the number?

SYLVIA. Well. Now—

CARL. A dutiful wife.

SYLVIA. Don't say such things. [*Into phone.*] May I speak to Mr. Temple— What? Is this Temple's Department Store? May I speak to Mr. Temple? He's in his office. This is Mrs. Temple. [*She looks at* CARL, *and purses her lips in a kiss to him.*] Hello, Tippy! Surprised? I'm calling you from the theatre. From the lounge. Well, it's between acts.

CARL. [*Calling.*] Tell him about the first act!

SYLVIA. [*Turning toward the phone as a sign for* CARL *not to talk.*] It's just another play, you might like it. Oh, Tip! You'll never guess who I bumped into here? Mr. Barrett. Yes, that's how I knew you were at the office, he said you had dinner together. Tip, I don't want you to work too late. Well, I thought you'd pick me up and we could go some place. Oh, you can't. [*She puts her tongue out at* CARL.] . . . Oh, Tip, Mr. Barrett's asked me to drop in at the Casino—he's with a party.

CARL. No! No! No!

SYLVIA. [*Turning her back to him again.*] So don't wait up for me in case I get home a little late.

CARL. [*Relaxing.*] Keep playing with the pretty fire, darling.

SYLVIA. Yes, dear, all right. Now don't work too hard. [*She kisses into the phone twice.*] Goodnight. [*She hangs up.*] Why didn't you shout louder, dear? Maybe he couldn't hear you?

CARL. I shouted as loudly as I could.

SYLVIA. [*Standing over him. Softly, as he takes her outstretched hand.*] Don't you want me to stay out late?

CARL. Of course I do. And when you go home to your husband I get so jealous I can't sleep all night.

SYLVIA. [*Softly.*] I'll send the chauffeur home.

CARL. [*Indicating doubt.*] Hm—hm!

SYLVIA. Then we can go after all.

CARL. Taking chances.

SYLVIA. It's all right. I'll have the door man get hold of him after the act.

CARL. What if Tippy boy decides to drop into the Casino himself? And finds we aren't there?

SYLVIA. [*Slightly nervous.*] Do you think he might?

CARL. [*Grinning, shaking his head.*] No. Tippy doesn't want to go to the Casino any more than we do. Do you know why Tippy's staying in his nice, big office this late, making believe he's working? Ask me why.

SYLVIA. Why?

CARL. Your husband, it seems, of all people is greatly enamoured of a young lady in his office. A filing clerk, I have been given to understand.

SYLVIA. No. You're fooling!

CARL. I bring you gospel truth.

SYLVIA. I can't believe it! Tippy!

CARL. We're not jealous, are we?

SYLVIA. I'm not jealous, honest I'm not. I really think I'm glad.

CARL. It eases your conscience.

SYLVIA. No, it's not that so much, although that's a little of it. [*She gropes.*] It's mostly that I feel Tippy and I are a little tired of each other, but he's a grand person, and if he's able to turn to other women I'm glad for him.

CARL. Well, that's it. This turning to other women hasn't been consummated as yet. It seems the young lady has objections.

SYLVIA. Poor Tippy.

CARL. She's a very difficult young lady. Tippy has kept her after hours three nights running now, on the pretext of work—fed her handsome dinners, in his office —coaxed her into drinking some excellent sherry— and that's all he's been able to accomplish.

SYLVIA. Poor, poor Tippy. He's such a rotten Casanova.

CARL. However, he reports things are looking up. They have gotten to the point where they are arguing over her submission, which is always a good sign, and it's only tonight that Tippy thinks he has better than a fighting chance.

SYLVIA. Good for Tippy!

CARL. In fact, the last thing Tippy informed me was that the young lady had an important errand to attend to and would come back to the office directly at the completion of said errand.

SYLVIA. Tippy and a filing clerk. That's amazing!

CARL. Don't you care, I love you.

SYLVIA. You do, don't you, Carl?

CARL. I do.

SYLVIA. [*Pathetically.*] It's the only thing I've got to cling to.

CARL. [*On a new tack.*] Sylvia, I've known a lot of girls. You know some of them. You've probably noticed I rarely hang around more than a month or two. I've long suspected it was a shortcoming of mine that I've never been able to fall in love, but I'm in love now, Sylvia.

SYLVIA. With me?

CARL. With you, Sylvia. I've told you that before, but it was just the thing to say.

SYLVIA. Yes, I understand.

CARL. Would you marry me?

SYLVIA. I'd rather than anything in the world. [*They kiss.*]

CARL. I'll be a very good husband. I'll try to be.

SYLVIA. I know you will.

CARL. You know you have a husband.

SYLVIA. Oh yes, I remember. A large robust one in a blue suit usually.

CARL. And spats.

SYLVIA. Does Tippy wear spats? Then I'll surely divorce him. That ought to be grounds enough.

CARL. No, you'll need other evidence.

SYLVIA. No, we won't. I'll go to Reno and establish residence. It doesn't take long. We'll be married before you know it. [*As she has talked she has put her hand to her breast, and now she looks for her clasp.*]

CARL. What's the matter?

SYLVIA. My clasp. My diamond clasp! I must have lost it!

CARL. I hope not.

SYLVIA. Tippy will have a fit.

CARL. Are you sure you were wearing it?

SYLVIA. Yes, I'm positive. [*She looks around.*] Damn. The big stone in the centre is practically an heirloom. Tippy's mother gave it to me for a wedding present. [*She stops, relieved.*] Oh, I remember now. I took it off in the car and fastened my collar with it. It's all right. It's on my coat.

CARL. And you checked it?

SYLVIA. Yes.

CARL. You'd better get it. I wouldn't leave it in a coat-room.

SYLVIA. Yes, I'd better.

CARL. I'll meet you here. Right after the intermission.

SYLVIA [*Smiling at him and wrinkling her nose.*] All right, Carl. [*She is off Left.* CARL *starts to exit Right.* EDDIE *passes him on the stairs, walking too quickly.* HE *goes directly to the Men's room.* CARL *is nearly at the top of the stairs before he reminds himself and calls to* EDDIE, *but too late.*]

CARL. Are you the coat-room boy? [*Without answering,* EDDIE *has walked the remaining few steps into the Men's room.* CARL *shrugs and exits. Now* EDDIE *comes into sight, looks at* CARL'S *exit, and runs quickly to his locker, Right. From his coat, which he opens as he runs, he takes the clasp. He takes a handkerchief from the pocket of the trousers in his locker, folds the pin in it, and replaces the handkerchief in the pocket. He is hardly finished when* MAE *enters, Left. She halts on the bottom step.*]

MAE. [*In an even, cold voice.*] Where've you been? [EDDIE *whirls around, frightened.*] The restaurant sent the coffee over themselves, they said you didn't come for it.

EDDIE. [*Nervously.*] Where is it?

MAE. It's upstairs. [EDDIE *starts quickly across stage toward Left.*] Better button your coat!

EDDIE. Oh! [*He almost leaps to correct himself.*]

MAE. [*Still deadly.*] What's the matter? Got a guilty

conscience? [*Significant pause.*] I should think you would have after the way you treated me. [*She turns,* EDDIE *following, looking up at her fearfully, registering her random remark.* HELEN *has appeared, Right, seen* EDDIE, *and drawn to the wall. On his exit* SHE *comes down, looking in her purse. She stops with a coin before the booth, sees the sign, notices the other phone, looks toward the entrance, and goes to it. She deposits the coin and dials.*]

HELEN. Mr. Temple, please. . . . Hello . . . I'm sorry you've been waiting, Mr. Temple. Yes, I'm alone. . . . I'd like to ask you a favor. Last night you said you'd be able to arrange a raise for me. That would be at least five dollars, wouldn't it? . . . Well, even if it was only five dollars that would be more than two hundred and fifty dollars a year. Mr. Temple, could you please give me two hundred dollars now, instead of the raise? You'd really be saving money. . . . No, it's not for me. . . . Thank you. . . . Could I please have it in cash? I need it tonight and these people wouldn't take a check. Please, Mr. Temple, you could get the money from petty cash in the safe. . . . Thank you. . . . Ask for Mr. White's room, Pennsylvania Hotel . . . I'll remember. . . . Right away. [*She hangs up and sinks onto the couch, Left.* EDDIE *comes down the Left stairs, goes to coffee table, placing tray on it. He turns and sees* HELEN.]

EDDIE. Why aren't you watching the show?

HELEN. I was watching it. I just came down.

EDDIE. [*Walking to* HELEN.] What's the matter, Helen?

HELEN. Kiss me, Eddie. [*He kisses her.*] Harder, so I can remember it. [*The three* USHERS *are coming down Left, and* MAE, *who is first, stops abruptly as she sees them kissing.* EDDIE *and* HELEN *separate.*]

ANNA. Don't move. Stand right there and I'll jump over you. [MAE, *without turning, looking fixedly at* EDDIE, *goes to table, with her tray.* HELEN *exits Left quickly.* ANNA *puts her dishes down on the same table as* KITTY. *A burst of applause is heard from above.*]

KITTY. There goes the curtain. We're late. [*The three* USHERS *take to filling the cups with coffee,* MAE *pouring.* EDDIE *takes his position back Right.*] Everything's mixed up tonight.

ANNA. [*To* MAE, *who has spilled coffee.*] Mae! You're spilling it. Say, you'd better let me pour. [THE TWELVE YEAR OLD GIRL *rushes down stage Left, and goes into Men's room by mistake, comes out very, very hurriedly and runs to Ladies'. The audience is beginning to come down from both staircases, including our necessary principals.*]

MA. If that cat's locked in the house for three days, it'll be terrible.

HERMAN. Oh, quit worrying. There'll be plenty for him to eat in the icebox.

MA. Oh, you and your jokes.

ANNA. [*To* HERMAN.] Coffee, sir? [HERMAN *takes it nervously, so does* MA.]

HERMAN. Thank you. What do you think of that, Ma —coffee.

MA. We'll get something for our money. I couldn't hear five words the fellow in the dress-suit was saying.

HERMAN. From where we were sitting I couldn't see anybody in a dress-suit. [EDDIE *comes forward with a lighter when he can.* JOHNSON *has come down and so has* CARL. JOHNSON *accepts coffee.* CARL *does not, but smokes.* JOHNSON *finds himself next to* CARL.]

JOHNSON. Hello. I can use this.

CARL. Any news yet.

JOHNSON. No, not yet.

CARL. You ought to be ashamed of yourself. Your wife having a baby and here you're out drinking.

JOHNSON. Say, a lot of husbands 'd be drinking more than coffee.

JOE. [*Who has entered Right with* MAKO, *the topcoat between them.*] I could think of something better to do on my last night in New York.

MAKO. You want to hear something? This is the first show I ever saw in my life.

MA. If I gave you coffee like this, you wouldn't touch it.

HERMAN. You know, the theatre don't pay for this. It's an advertisement for the coffee people.

MA. It is? What kind of coffee is it?

HERMAN. I don't know. You're supposed to tell from the taste.

MRS. MADISON. [*45 years of age, well dressed, beautiful face.*] How do you like the big city?

DONALD. [*Who isn't having too good a time.*] Oh, it's all right.

MRS. MADISON. Were you surprised to find that your brother and I were married?

DONALD. Well, I was sort of surprised.

STANLEY MADISON. [*A blonde young man in tails.*] How do you like the show, Don?

MRS. MADISON. It's a little different from Alabama.

DONALD. Say, we got shows in Alabama. We got the best burlesque house in the South. I like burlesque.

MRS. MADISON. A very intelligent form of art.

STANLEY. We'll go to one later on in the week. [MRS. MADISON *has looked at him.*] If I'm not busy. [FRANK, SYLVIA'S *chauffeur, in uniform, has been looking for* SYLVIA *and spies her.*]

SYLVIA. Oh, Frank.

FRANK. The door man said you wanted to see me, ma'm.

SYLVIA. Yes, I was going to send you home. But my diamond pin is missing. Will you look very carefully in the car, and if it's not there, look in the coat-room. I'll wait here for you. It must be on the floor some place.

FRANK. Yes, ma'm [*He exits, Left.*]

CARL. [*Burlesquing surprise.*] Mrs. Temple! How are you?

SYLVIA. [*Overdoing it just as much, extending her hand.*] Why, Mr. Barrett, Junior! Isn't this a coincidence? Whom are you with?

CARL. I happen to be alone. I don't know— I just felt like seeing this show tonight.

SYLVIA. So did I. Isn't it a small world?

CARL. I've often said that.

MAKO. Say, what do these people do in the daytime?

JOE. They got jobs. They're not all rich. [MAKO *has put a cigarette in his mouth.* EDDIE *comes forward and lights it. This is a surprise to* MAKO *who looks him over, grins slightly, and shakes his head at* JOE *in amusement.*]

[*The chatter is slightly louder as the curtain descends slowly.*]

CURTAIN

ACT TWO

ACT TWO

*Scene: The curtain rises on almost the scene
we left. Some persons have changed positions,
some are missing. Most persons have finished
coffee, the ushers are gathering up cups.* ED-
DIE *still lights cigarettes when he can. Chatter.
The* TWELVE YEAR OLD GIRL *comes out of
Ladies' and runs upstairs.*

MA *and* HERMAN *are seated on couch Left at
rise of curtain.*

MA. Why should you spend three dollars and thirty
cents to see a play when they always make a moving
picture out of it and you can see it for a quarter?

HERMAN. [*Still drinking coffee.*] They leave a lot of
things out. Plays are always dirtier than pictures.

MA. Why are they?

HERMAN. I once read about it. The people who go see
plays are more intelligent than people who go to see
movies. [*He sips.*] And there aren't any censors.

MRS. MADISON. Personally, I'd rather go home. But if
we're to go any place it ought to be Harlem.

STANLEY. What do you say, Donald, it's the only place
to go in New York.

DONALD. [*Southern accent.*] I'm only a guest. But if you think going to Harlem is a novelty to a native of Alabama you're all mistaken. [*They laugh.*]

JOE. [*Who is standing with* MAKO, *looking at his watch.*] If we get out of here right now, we can just catch the last show at the Paramount.

MAKO. I saw it.

JOE. You did?

MAKO. Yep.

JOE. How did you have the nerve to go to a movie? Weren't you afraid of being picked up?

MAKO. Safest place is a crowd.

JOE. [*He shakes his head.*] Picture any good?

MAKO. I didn't like it. [*He looks at him.*] It's a prison picture.

JOE. Oh!

SLYVIA. [*Looking toward the head of the staircase, Right.*] I hope Frank has found the pin.

CARL. It's insured, isn't it?

SYLVIA. Yes, of course it's insured, but you don't know how the Temple family values that darn thing. I'm going to see what's happened to him. I'll see you here later.

CARL. [*Smiles meaningly.*] Later. [*She starts quickly, through the people, Left.*]

JOHNSON. [*Next to* CARL.] It's a pretty long intermission, isn't it? [*The buzzer sounds, there is the concerted movement to put out cigarettes and start upstairs.*]

CARL. I beg your pardon?

JOHNSON. I just said it was a pretty long intermission and it rang. [JOHNSON *goes into the Men's room.*]

EDDIE. Curtain going up! Curtain going up!

JOE. Let's finish this, huh?

MAKO. Sure. Let's sit down, I like it here. [EVERYONE *is exiting Right and Left, except* JOE *and* MAKO, *who remain seated. The three* USHERS *are gathering the cups and tidying.* HERMAN *puts down his cup but it overturns, spilling.*]

HERMAN. Oh! Excuse me! I'm sorry!

EDDIE. That's all right, sir. [*He takes a napkin and begins to wipe it up.* [MA *and* HERMAN *beat an embarrassed retreat. As the* MADISON *party is starting up the stairs Right,* GEORGE *is hastily coming down.* GEORGE *is in a business suit, and the same age as* STANLEY. *He brushes past him, they turn, recognize each other.*]

STANLEY. Nelson!

GEORGE. Madison! [*They shake hands vigorously, disturbing traffic.*]

STANLEY. [*Animated.*] I haven't seen you since graduation.

GEORGE. That's right.

STANLEY. [*Reminding himself.*] This is Mrs. Madison; this is my brother, Donald. [*They* ALL *mumble "How do you do's."*]

MRS. MADISON. Stanley, we're blocking traffic.

STANLEY. I'll see you after the next act!

GEORGE. Right here!

STANLEY. Don't forget! Down here! [*They exit, Right.*
GEORGE *goes toward phone.*] We went to Alabama U.
together. He was on the swimming team— [*They are
out.* GEORGE *puts his nickel in the slot and dials. The
stage is now cleared except for* EDDIE, *the* USHERS, JOE
and MAKO.]

MAE. [*At the coffee table. This is the first time she and*
EDDIE *have been this close during this act.*] You must
feel pretty popular—two girls fighting over you. [EDDIE
says nothing. MAE *will exit Left.* ANNA *and* KITTY *will
enter Ladies' with the cups.*]

GEORGE. [*Into phone.*] Hello, Jean. I just called up to
tell you it looks like a tough session, and you'd better
not expect me until late. . . . Well, this is no holiday
for me either, having to work like this. . . . You just
tell your mother I have to work, she can understand
that, can't she? . . . I'll talk to her, put her on. . . .
[*Too nicely.*] Hello, Mother Woodruff, how do you
feel? I'm sorry I couldn't be home the one night you
visit us, but you know, business . . . I resent that! Listen here, you haven't any right . . . I'm working! . . .
[EDDIE *has been emptying ash trays again.*] Go 'head,
call me back. I'm at the boss' house. [*He looks and
reads.*] The number is Circle—7–4196. [*He hangs up,
looks at the phone, puts his hands in his pockets, and
paces stage Right and Left.* JOHNSON *comes out of
Men's room and goes to the phone.* EDDIE *exits Left.*]
Excuse me, Mac. I'm expecting a call on this phone—
it'll only take a minute.

JOHNSON. Oh, that's all right. [*He sits, taking out a*

cigarette and lighting it. GEORGE *is getting impatient.*
He looks at the phone, then toward the stairs. He starts
to walk away from the phone. He pauses at the foot
of the stairs, Right. Suddenly disgusted he mumbles,
"Nuts," and runs up. JOHNSON, *oblivious, gets up, gets*
his nickel out and is about to put it in when it rings,
frightening him. He answers it.] Hello? Who? No
ma'm, this is the Forty-Third Street Theatre.

MAKO. [*Putting out his hand.*] Say! [*But he is too*
late. JOHNSON *has spilled the beans, and has not heard*
MAKO. MAKO *relaxes,* JOE *smiles.*]

JOHNSON. [*Continuing.*] I'm Mr. Johnson, but you
wouldn't know me. . . . [*Looking at number.*] Yes
ma'm, you have the right number. . . . Why,
MADAM! [*He hangs up, shaking his head, and puts*
his nickel in, dialing.]

MAKO. I wouldn't want to be in that feller's shoes. [*And*
as an afterthought.] And I guess he wouldn't want to
be in mine either, heh?

JOHNSON. [*Into phone.*] The fourth floor, please . . .
Could I please speak to Mister Neil. . . . Hello, Sam,
how is it? . . . Isn't it taking a long time? . . .
You've been telling me ten minutes for the last two
hours. . . . I am at the theatre! Sam, do you know if
they gave Ruth ether? . . . Sam, if it's too painful tell
the doctor I said to give her ether. . . . Well, I
thought maybe the husband has to give permission.
. . . Maybe I ought to come down. . . . All right, I'll
stay here. I'll call you back in ten minutes. [*He hangs*
up and goes slowly Left, out, dejected.]

JOE. Want to go up?

MAKO. [*Shaking his head negatively.*] That having a kid must be a funny feeling—I mean for the man, too.

JOE. Everybody goes through it.

MAKO. Not me! All my life I knew I wouldn't have a kid, I had a hunch. I thought maybe I'd get married sometime, I could imagine that— [*A large effort to be jovial.*]—but I guess I ain't got much time to even get married now. You got to have a day off to get the license. And I ain't got the day. [JOE *says nothing, just looks at him.* MAKO *starts anew, anxious to keep talking.*] Say, I guess I'm lucky I ain't got a kid. How'd I feel? [*Suddenly.*] You got any kids?

JOE. I got a girl. She's thirteen years old.

MAKO. No kidding! Thirteen years!

JOE. She graduates public school the day after tomorrow. You're not supposed to graduate until you're fourteen, but she's skipped twice. Smart as a whip.

MAKO. Say, I'll bet you're excited.

JOE. If I didn't have to take you on this little trip I'd be at her graduation. She's going to play the violin.

MAKO. I'm sorry, Taft, if it's up to me we can postpone this trip. [JOE *laughs softly, then is quiet. So is* MAKO.]

JOE. Tony, I'd like to ask you something. [MAKO *looks at him.*] If you don't feel like talking just tell me and I'll shut up.

MAKO. What is it?

JOE. You know, every cop in New York City knew

you were in town. And the last three days we even knew
you were in the Times Square district. What was the
idea in breaking out of jail two thousand miles away
and coming to the one spot you were sure to be picked
up?

MAKO. Pretty dumb, eh? Sometimes I wonder myself.
When I was in jail—I only wanted one thing. I wanted
to kill myself! I used to wake up in the middle of the
night—screamin'. All day long I'd be in a cold sweat—
it'd come right through my clothes. Soaking wet. I
thought if I could only knock myself off in a hurry—
that's all I wanted. Once I tried it.

JOE. You did?

MAKO. I planned it all out. I cut my hand on a bed-spring
and the doctor came in with iodine. That's what I was
waiting for. I grabbed the iodine and swallowed it.
[*He shakes his head.*] There wasn't enough of it; all I
got was a belly-ache. [*He leans back.* JOE *watches him
intently.*] You think I'm a coward? Once I killed four
guys, by myself. [*He smiles.*] That's all right, I was
allowed to kill 'em. There was a war going on. That's
how I got to be a citizen. I was in the army and I got
a medal.

JOE. I didn't know that.

MAKO. My lawyer thought that would be a good thing
to tell in court and he was all ready to spring it—and
then he found out that the foreman of the jury had a
bad war record—he was a slacker—so we let it go.

JOE. That's tough.

MAKO. I'm no coward. I thought about getting knocked

off lots of times. I figured maybe I'd get shot sometime.
Well, I thought I wouldn't mind that, if it was quick.
Or maybe the electric chair. That didn't seem so bad.
But hanging— I never counted on that. I used to sit in
that jail and hold my hand over my mouth to stop
breathing. Did you ever try it? You feel your eyes are
gonna pop out of your head in another second and you
gotta grab your hand away. I used to try and keep my
hand there just that extra second—to see how much it
hurt—but I couldn't do it.

JOE. You were torturing yourself.

TONY. I was going nuts. And then I said to myself,
What the hell, I'll try to get out of here. What'll they
do about it, shoot me in the back? I'd thank 'em, that'd
be a favor!

JOE. And you got out.

MAKO. Yeah, they double-crossed me—nobody shot me.

JOE. Why didn't you stay away from New York?

MAKO. Yeah, that's the funny part. Once I got out I
didn't want to die any more. But I knew I was gonna
get caught, sooner or later. Then I wanted one more
thing. I wanted to fix somebody, and he was in New
York.

JOE. You should have stayed away.

MAKO. Say, you can imagine how much I hated this
son of— I just wanted to see him dead, right in front
of me, and then I didn't care what happened. If I
couldn't kill myself before they grabbed me, all right
—I wouldn't mind hanging any more. I used to pray

to God—and I ain't religious—to let me get even—
that's all I wanted. I didn't ask for any heaven or any
of that stuff—I just wanted to kill this one bastard.
Kill him by myself.

JOE. Who was it, Tony?

MAKO. [*Who has been speaking with a controlled in-
tensity, mostly for his own benefit, lost in a great vin-
dictive fire, comes back to earth.*] You know him. Anderson.

JOE. Anderson. Wasn't he a friend of yours?

MAKO. I just knew him. He used to hang around Goldie's. He went with us out west, the boys had an idea
about something out there that didn't pan out. On the
way back we ran out of money and I stuck up a gas
station. There was one old guy in it, he must've been
nuts. I had the gun on him and he turns his back on
me to grab ahold of a shot-gun in the corner. [*He
shakes his head sadly at the memory.*] When we got
back here everything went smooth for a couple of weeks
and then I get picked up for this gas station job in
Colorado. I didn't even know it was Colorado.

JOE. And Anderson told on you?

MAKO. He didn't have to, mind you! Nobody picked
him up! He just wanted to get a reward of a couple
of hundred bucks and he squealed. Sold me out; he
knew he was hanging me—all for a couple of hundred
bucks!

JOE. Couldn't you get ahold of him in all that time you
were here? You know he hangs out in Goldie's.

MAKO. He didn't stay at Goldie's! He beat it. He was afraid of me! He read in the paper I was out and he knew I'd come for him! I found out he was hiding in his wife's apartment—but nobody knew where it was. [*Proudly.*] So I got all the Andersons out of the telephone book and I started around. Dressed like a letter-carrier!

JOE. Yeah. Where'd you get that letter-carrier's uniform?

MAKO. I rented it. I said I was going to a party.

JOE. That uniform was clever; it was just like a pass.

MAKO. [*Leaning back again, the fire spent.*] It wasn't clever enough, though. I still had twenty Andersons to go when I got picked up. [ANNA *and* KITTY *come out of Ladies'*—MAKO *watching them idly.* JOE *notices* MAKO *following their legs with his eyes as they cross and exit Right upstairs.*]

JOE. [*Looking at his watch.*] Listen, Tony, our train doesn't leave for three hours. If you feel like it we can go to a hotel—there's a dame hangs around the station —I can get her number from one of the boys.

MAKO. No. Thanks, Taft.

JOE. Are you feeling sick again?

MAKO. I'm all right. You're a white guy for a cop, and few of 'em are. Just let's talk, what do you say? I haven't talked to anybody so long I'm full of gab.

JOE. All right.

MAKO. What about your kid?

JOE. What about her?

MAKO. What are you giving her for a present?

JOE. You mean for a graduation present? Well, my wife's made her a dress—a regular ladies' dress—like an evening gown—but on a small scale. And I'm buying her ladies' shoes with high heels—say, she'll be crazy about it.

MAKO. I don't know. That's no present for a kid—getting clothes. I used to get birthday presents like that. My mother used to starve herself and get me a couple of handkerchiefs or a shirt. I didn't like that. I remember once I wanted an electric train. Geez, I wanted that train. Do you know what I got that Christmas? A suit of woolen underwear! I was nuts about machinery. Maybe if my folks had enough dough to buy me things I wouldn't 've learned to pick pockets for 'em. [*He breaks off from this mush.*] No, a dress ain't no present.

JOE. A girl thinks a lot of clothes.

MAKO. [*Reaching into his pants pocket.*] Say, listen. I got about six hundred bucks here. You want to do me a favor?

JOE. Don't be crazy.

MAKO. Now what am I gonna blow this dough on? You take five hundred and get the kid something from me.

JOE. I don't need any money!

MAKO. [*Pushing it in his hand.*] Now listen, Taft. I'd rather your kid get this than some crook warden. Come on. I got no one to give it to. [*He continues pushing it in* JOE's *palm.*] You know I'm right. That's it.

JOE. Thanks. It's a lot of money, Tony . . . [*He takes out his cigarette case and puts the bills in it.*]

MAKO. You keep money in a cigarette case?

JOE. I wouldn't want this to get lost. What should I buy with it?

MAKO. Yeah, let's see. [*He puts the rest of his money back in his pocket.*] What did I always want? She don't like machinery, huh?

JOE. [*Putting the case in his coat pocket, nearest* TONY.] Well—she's a girl—

MAKO. You better put that in your other pocket. I'll lift it on you.

JOE. [*Laughing.*] That's O.K. I trust you.

MAKO. I'll forget myself. I'm the best pick-pocket you've ever seen. Now what can we get your kid? How about a stack of dolls?

JOE. She's a little too old for that.

MAKO. All the dames I know ask for jewelry. You can't get much for five hundred, but you can get something. Maybe a— [*He pantomimes a necklace.*] with a couple of little diamonds.

JOE. Well—if you want me to—except she's only a kid—

MAKO. Say! I got it! You remember I was just telling you about that electric train? If somebody had come up to me and asked me if I wanted the Brooklyn Bridge or that train I'd have taken the train. Well, she wants something like that, too. We'll give it to her.

JOE. An electric train?

MAKO. [*Disgusted with him.*] No. She don't want a train. She's a girl; she's got something else in her mind. You go up to her and just say this: Baby, what do you want? Anything in the whole world, I'll get it for you. You'll see it won't even be five hundred bucks.

JOE. That's a good idea. She'll be getting something she wants.

MAKO. Even if it's something nutty, get it. Say, if anybody had said that to me, I'd remember it all my life. [*Seriously.*] Only don't get her nothing that'll make her sick, like cake or a lot of bananas. One time I got murdered on a dozen bananas.

JOE. This is very nice of you, Tony.

MAKO. Better not tell her who it's from.

JOE. I'll tell her it's from an uncle out west.

MAKO. [*He grins.*] Yeah, from Colorado.

JOE. If there's anything I can do for you, Tony—if there's something you want—

MAKO. No—you can't do anything. I'd like two things to happen. First, I'd like to get Anderson in a dark alley for a couple of minutes; and second, after that—I'd like to drop dead. [*He turns slowly to* JOE, *who has been looking at him.*] You couldn't fix that, could you? [*He laughs shortly, bitterly.* JOE *looks at him pathetically. There is loud laughter from upstairs.* MAKO *looks upwards.*] Let's go upstairs. I want to watch that little dog on the stage.

JOE. [*Getting up with him. They talk as they cross to exit Right.*] What little dog?

MAKO. Didn't you see that little dog on the sofa the fat actress brought in? I been watching it all the time, expecting it to pull something. [MAKO *and* JOE *have just started up the Right stairs, and* MAE *comes down. She is looking at her footing as she passes the pair, who have started up necessarily abreast.* MAKO *has stopped involuntarily and stares at her.* MAE *has been oblivious of this and continues on her march to Ladies' room.*]

JOE. [*As* MAE *enters Ladies' room. Feeling that* MAKO *has stopped and seeing him stare at her back. Quietly.*] What's the matter? Do you know her?

MAKO. [*Turning back quickly. In a strange, excited voice.*] No—no—I don't know her. [MAE *comes out of Ladies' room—goes to coffee table. They both exit,* MAKO *throwing one more glance back.* MAE *takes all the wafers out of the box and puts them on the tray. She goes to throw the box in the wastebasket and comes back to arrange the crackers on the dishes.* CARL *comes down stage, Left. He crosses to a sofa where he sits, looking at* MAE, *whose back is to him, and whose short starched skirt reveals an attractive expanse of hose. He takes out a cigarette. As he lights it* MAE, *knowing he is behind her, shifts her position so that she can see him. She catches him staring at her.* HE *smiles,* SHE *smiles.*]

MAE. [*For a girl in her frame of mind, too sweetly.*] Don't you like the show?

CARL. Yes, I like it fine. But I've seen it.

MAE. Do you always see shows twice?

CARL. This time I'm seeing it for a friend. [MAE *laughs too heartily,* CARL *joins in.* CARL *is willing to keep this up.*] Have you seen it yet?

MAE. Oh yes. About a hundred times.

CARL. What do you do on your day off? See another show?

MAE. Well, there aren't any shows open on Sunday. [*She smiles.*] But I usually end up at a picture.

CARL. I wouldn't call that much of a day off.

MAE. [*Sadly.*] I know. But you get awfully lonely by yourself. I don't know anybody in New York.

CARL. Why, I don't believe that. A girl as pretty as you are—you must have two dozen young men on the string.

MAE. [*Wistfully.*] Thanks—but I'm afraid not. I haven't had a date since I left Rhode Island. And that's more than a year ago.

CARL. You're making me feel ashamed of myself.

MAE. You?

CARL. Certainly. I'm a citizen of New York and this is no way for us to treat a good-looking girl from Delaware.

MAE. Rhode Island. [*They both force a little laugh.*]

CARL. Do you live all alone? [MAE *nods.*] And you're

off on Sundays? [*She nods again and* CARL *would say something, but notices* SYLVIA *coming down, Left.* MAE *can see from his expression that he knows* SYLVIA, *and moves away.* SYLVIA *goes to* CARL *after a puzzled sideglance at* MAE *and talks in a low voice to keep out of earshot.* MAE *putters another second and exits Left.*]

SYLVIA. The clasp is gone, Carl.

CARL. It is?

SYLVIA. I looked all over. It was on the collar. I remember opening it and then fastening it again.

CARL. Maybe you put it in your purse.

SYLVIA. No, I recall it distinctly now. I couldn't get the safety catch closed and I used my nail file to turn it.

CARL. That coat room boy must have taken it.

SYLVIA. I imagine so. What shall I do?

CARL. Did you say anything to him?

SYLVIA. I just said I lost it and he helped me look. He did seem awfully nervous.

CARL. He has it, and you can get it back by frightening him. Just demand it and threaten to call the police.

SYLVIA. Maybe he didn't take it. He's only a boy—

CARL. He has it; don't be so soft-hearted.

SYLVIA. [*Who has been looking at him adoringly. The pin is not much in her life.* SHE *seats herself and talks.*] Look how he bosses me already. Carl, I've been thinking. Will you do me a big favor?

CARL. I might.

SYLVIA. It will be the only favor I'll ever ask of you.

CARL. What is it?

SYLVIA. Please be with me when I tell Tippy about the divorce.

CARL. Oh!

SYLVIA. Please, darling. He'll think so much more of us. He'll understand, I know Tippy. If we go to him honestly and tell him we're really in love, he'll want us to be happy. I know he will.

CARL. I guess so. But before you make any leaps and bounds you'll regret, you better know just how I'm situated.

SYLVIA. Oh, darling, I don't care. You don't have to confess anything.

CARL. You're sweet.

SYLVIA. You're not somebody's father, are you?

CARL. No—

SYLVIA. Then it's all right.

CARL. But it's father trouble—

SYLVIA. Oh! Your father. He won't like me—a divorcee.

CARL. I don't think so. In fact I'm pretty sure of it. You see, father's always had me pretty much under his thumb, with my being dependent on him.

SYLVIA. [Addressing his locks.] Sweet.

CARL. I'm just an old veteran man-about-town.

SYLVIA. Carl, if you can't support me in the manner to which I'm accustomed I'll only eat two meals a day.

CARL. That wouldn't solve it—

SYLVIA. One meal! Just some old toast!

CARL. That'll help a little. I'm pretty practical, Sylvia, though you'd never suspect it, and I've considered this very carefully. I've no money, no prospects of earning any, and a father who'd stop my allowance just as soon as not. In fact, it just occurs to me—I'm in debt besides.

SYLVIA. Why did I fall in love with such a wastrel?

CARL. That's the point, dear. And now that I've painted myself as black as I really am—do you still want the wastrel?

SYLVIA. [*Cocking her head, looking at him from side to side.*] Well now, let me see? [*She considers.*] Mmmmm, yes, I'll have him.

CARL. Thank you. [*He kisses her.*] Now here's what I've thought out, all by myself. Instead of you going to Reno, you get a divorce right here in New York.

SYLVIA. But how can we?

CARL. You'll have no trouble getting evidence— Tippy has an apartment at the Pennsylvania Hotel, and a very nice filing clerk.

SYLVIA. But darling, we couldn't do a thing like that.

CARL. We'll have to. Even a small property settlement will keep these fingers from getting dish-washy for a long, long time. [*He has been holding her hands and now he kisses her finger-tips.*]

SYLVIA. [*Quietly.*] You're not serious!

CARL. Darling. I know it sounds terrible right now—but the money means nothing to Tippy—he wouldn't even notice it. You're certainly entitled to it; and to us—well, it's just the difference between being able to get married or—or not.

SYLVIA. But on Tippy's money—we wouldn't want to live on that?

CARL. What else is there to do? I haven't any money of my own, and if father even suspected I wanted to marry you he'd throw me out. [*He notices* SYLVIA's *reaction.*] Darling, it isn't that terrible.

SYLVIA. Catching Tippy in a hotel room—that's so cheap.

CARL. You're making it much worse than it is, and it's really the only solution. Tippy can certainly afford a few hundred thousand—father'll be able to throw me out to his heart's content, and we can live abroad until the whole thing dies down—

SYLVIA. [*Gets up from the couch, walks to foot of stairs Right.*] No, Carl, I don't think so—

CARL. Darling, don't make any decision now. I think you've been a little shocked; by tomorrow you won't think it's too horrible.

SYLVIA. That's what I'm afraid of, so I'd better decide now. I know my code of ethics must look funny to you, but it's the only code I've got. God knows I've little else.

CARL. Honey, in a month from now we'll laugh at this—

SYLVIA. [*Keeping on, in a tired, even voice.*] I didn't mind being unfair to Tippy, not too much, because I knew I loved you. I didn't feel I was cheapening myself. But to deliberately connive to get some of Tippy's money to support you— No, Carl. [*She shakes her head.*] I love you, really I do, but I don't love you that much. I couldn't love anybody that much.

CARL. [*Gets up, goes to* SYLVIA.] Let's not discuss it any more. I'll see you tomorrow—for lunch some place—

SYLVIA. No. No more hiding. I'd give anything in the world if tonight hadn't happened—if you hadn't told me you loved me so much you wanted to marry me. That's funny, isn't it? [MAKO *and* JOE *are coming down stage Right, quickly.* CARL *and* SYLVIA *have stopped talking when they have entered the scene. When they pass her, she suddenly averts her head and runs up the stairs.*]

CARL. Sylvia, wait a minute. [HE *sees that she does not intend to stop.* HE *goes up after her slowly.* MAKO *and* JOE *go as far as the door of the Men's room where* JOE *unlocks the handcuffs, waiting for* MAKO *outside. He crosses to the small center table for a wafer as* MAC *comes down Left.* MAC *will take coffee and crackers.*]

MAC. Where you taking the Eyetalian, Joe?

JOE. Colorado.

MAC. Colorado? Say, that's a long trip.

JOE. I'm only taking him as far as Chicago. I meet one of the Colorado boys there and turn him over. [*He looks toward the Men's room.*] He's a pretty sick dago right now.

MAC. How do you sleep at night, guarding a criminal? Aren't you afraid he'll jump off the train?

JOE. You put a sleeping powder in his coffee.

MAC. No!

JOE. [*Chuckles as he remembers.*] No, but it sounds like a good idea. One of the boys tried it and he had the coffee switched on him—he slept for two days.

MAC. [*Chuckles.*] What are they going to try him for?

JOE. He's been tried. He escaped.

MAC. Is that so? He looked like such a harmless feller. You certainly never can tell. What was he sent up for?

JOE. Murder. They're hanging him a day after he gets off the train.

MAC. No! What do you think of that? He was standing close alongside of me—up there—talking— I thought he was just a friend of yours. I kept kidding about you hanging around with crooks so much you'd get bad habits—and then I went to light his cigarette and he held up his arm and I saw the handcuff! [*He shakes his head.*] Gee—I should think you'd be afraid to leave him there alone for fear he would get away again.

JOE. I would be if I hadn't looked it over first. How is he going to get out of there?

MAC. I thought maybe you might be afraid of the window.

JOE. What window? There's no window in there!

MAC. Yes, there is, up high, a little one—it's painted over. [*There is a crash of glass from the Men's room.*]

JOE. [*Drawing his gun as he runs into Men's room.*] Mako! Come back here! [*We hear two shots. He rushes back and goes to the telephone booth. He sees the "Out of Order" sign, and mutters.*] God damn! [*He turns and rushes to the wall phone.* MAC, *who has been jittery, follows him.*]

MAC. Joe, what happened? Is he shot? Where is he? Did he get away?

JOE. Give me the Forty-Seventh Street police station! Hurry it!

MAC. [*Getting no response from* JOE, *he looks toward the Men's room. As though to protect himself, he reaches for his gun, and finds it missing.*] Joe! My gun! It's gone! Somebody's picked my pocket!

JOE. [*Turning.*] Are you sure? [*He whirls back to the phone.*] Let me talk to Captain Seaver . . . Seaver! This is Joe Taft . . . Tony Mako just got away. Mako! He got out of the Men's room of the Forty-Third Street Theatre. He isn't off the block yet. He jumped out of the window. . . . He had on a blue suit, no hat, no overcoat, and he's got a pair of handcuffs on his left wrist. Listen, send a man up to Goldie's, the pool hall. Anderson hangs around there and Mako is out to kill him. He'll go there, and listen—I think he's got a gun . . . Forty-Third Street Theatre. [*He hangs up and turns on* MAC.] Is there any way to get off that roof next door?

MAC. [*Dazed.*] The roof!

JOE. [*Almost shouting, to get* MAC *out of his reverie.*] I think he started up that fire escape! Is there any way to get off that roof?

MAC. There's another fire escape on the other side of the building.

JOE. [*Starting to run, grabbing* MAC—*both exiting Left.*] Show me it! Come on! Hurry, will you? [*All quiet.* JOHNSON *comes down slowly from Right. When he is at the foot of the stairs* EDDIE *appears at the top and speaks.*]

EDDIE. Is anything the matter?

JOHNSON. What?

EDDIE. Did you call?

JOHNSON. I wasn't saying anything. I'm just going to use the telephone. [JOHNSON *inserts his coin and dials phone on wall.*] The fourth floor, please. . . . Could I please speak to Mister Neil? . . . Hello, Sam, how is it? . . . [*Anxiously.*] Why is it taking so long? . . . [*Suddenly.*] Sam! What's wrong? You're hiding something from me! [*Wildly.*] Sam! What's the matter with Ruth! . . . [*Quietly.*] The doctor? I'll talk to him. . . . What's the matter, doctor? . . . A Cæsarian? Isn't that dangerous? Does she have to have it? . . . All right, doctor, if you think so. . . . Doctor, couldn't I come down there? I won't be in the way . . . all right, I'll stay here. . . . Listen, doctor, if you need any extra nurses or anything please get them. I don't care about the expense, I'll pay anything it costs. I've got money, and I've got friends who'll lend me as much as you want. Doctor, I don't want you to take any

chances with my wife. My wife comes first—don't
sacrifice my wife for the baby. I don't want the baby if
it'll cost me my wife. . . . Please, doctor, I'm trusting
you. . . . Thank you. God bless you. Thank you,
doctor. [JOHNSON *hangs up slowly. He runs his hand
over his face and wipes his eyes and turns to exit,
Right. Right now, from the drapes of the Men's door,
we see* MAKO'S *head. He draws back as* JOHNSON *stops.*
JOHNSON *starts in his direction, slowly, lost in his own
thoughts, and turns toward the water fountain after
having almost gone by it on the way to the Men's
room. He drinks shortly, wipes his mouth dully, and
turns and exits, Right.* MAKO *pops out. He is slightly
disheveled. In his right hand is the gun. His left arm
hangs limply, his hand and the handcuffs are wet with
blood. He is tense, cat-like, deadly. Just as he goes to
the booth, he sees the "Out of Order" sign and stops
short. He had forgotten about it. He mutters something
in Italian, looks at the dial phone, the head of the stairs,
and runs to it, his left arm dangling grotesquely. He
puts the gun under his left armpit, takes a coin from his
pocket, inserts it and dials. He looks nervously to the
head of the stairs. When he talks he tries to disguise
his voice, speaking higher and slower.*]

MAKO. Is this Goldie's Pool Room? Is Mister Anderson there? Could I please speak to him? . . . [*From
his breast pocket he takes his handkerchief and hastily
puts it over the mouthpiece. Still, he maintains his altered voice.*] Hello, Mister Anderson? I work at the
Forty-Third Street Theatre, with your wife. She wants
you to come down here right away. . . . No, I don't
know what it is, but she said it was very important and

for you to come down to the theatre as quick as you could. . . . Yes. . . . She'll be downstairs in the smoking room, waiting for you. . . . O.K. Mr. Anderson. You're welcome. [*He hangs up quickly, his eyes dart to the stairs above him, where he sees the* TWELVE YEAR OLD GIRL *coming down, and running into the Ladies' room. As she disappears, he runs toward the Men's room, but stops at the door, and looks about. An idea hits him. He runs to the phone booth, enters it and shuts it. We see him sink down under the glass partition out of sight. From Right,* EDDIE *and* CARL *come down.* CARL *has* EDDIE *gently by the arm, and* EDDIE *keeps looking up at him nervously. The* TWELVE YEAR OLD GIRL *runs out of the Ladies' room and exits, Right. At the foot of the stairs* EDDIE *cannot restrain himself further.*]

EDDIE. What's the matter?

CARL. [*Patiently, too kindly.*] Son, I want you to know I'm your friend. I just don't like to see a young fellow like you do anything you'll regret the rest of your life.

EDDIE. [*Nervously.*] I don't know what you're talking about.

CARL. Yes, you do. [*He takes* EDDIE *by both shoulders.*] Look me in the eye, boy.

EDDIE. [*Defensively.*] I haven't done anything.

CARL. Give it back. I promise no harm will come to you.

EDDIE. Give what back? I haven't got anything of yours.

CARL. My wife's. That diamond pin.

EDDIE. A diamond pin! How would I have it? You can search me if you want to. Go 'head, search me!

CARL. [*Still kindly.*] You took it from her coat. You haven't it on you. Take my advice, son. I'm older than you are. Just get it and give it to me and we'll both forget this incident.

EDDIE. I haven't got it, I tell you!

CARL. [*Firmer.*] Listen, boy, I'll tell you the truth. I've already phoned for the police and they're on their way over here. But I saw how young you were and I took pity on you. Now this is your last chance. Are you going to be fool enough to go to prison or are you going to give me the pin? [EDDIE *is bluffed, and a little too dazed to answer.* CARL *follows up his advantage, speaking kindly again.* SYLVIA *comes down Right, noiseless on the carpet, unseen by* CARL *who has his back on her.*] Just to be sure you don't get in trouble we won't even tell my wife. I'll take charge of it, and you keep on pretending you haven't found it. Now give me the pin and I'll give it to her at home. You can trust me. [EDDIE *sees* SYLVIA *standing stock still at the top of the stairs, and* CARL *turns to see what* EDDIE *is looking at. He doesn't lose his composure for a second. The jig is up, he merely smiles at her.* SYLVIA *starts toward* EDDIE, *not even looking at* CARL.]

SYLVIA. I couldn't have believed that.

CARL. [*Easily.*] He'll give you back the pin, dear.

SYLVIA. [*Quietly.*] Have you got my pin?

EDDIE. [*Desperately, breaking.*] I didn't know it was yours, madam. I found it on the floor and put it away.

SYLVIA. All right. Give it to me. [SYLVIA *sits on couch,*

her face averted from CARL'S. EDDIE *turns and goes to his locker, from which he will get the pin.*]

CARL. Ashamed of me?

SYLVIA. I'm ashamed of myself. [*From Left* MAC *and* CAPTAIN SEAVER *come down.* SEAVER *is a heavy-set, capable-looking officer. He wears civilian clothes and a felt hat.* MAC *is talking as they come down the stairs.* EDDIE, *who has the pin, and who has started to cross with it from his locker to* SYLVIA, *stops dead at seeing* SEAVER. *This must be the "police" whom* CARL *said he called.*]

MAC. Please try to keep this quiet, Captain. It'll give the show a bad name. We've never had the police in this theatre before.

SEAVER. Where is he?

EDDIE. [*Who has gone right to* SEAVER. *Blurting it out.*] I found it, I didn't steal it. [*He holds the pin out for* SEAVER *to take.*] I was only taking care of it!

SEAVER. What!

MAC. What's the matter, Eddie?

SEAVER. [*Taking the pin.*] Whose is this? What's all this about?

EDDIE. I don't know. I swear I didn't take it off a coat! I found it on the floor!

SYLVIA. It's my pin. It was missing from my coat.

CARL. [*Goes toward* SEAVER.] Let me explain this. This young man, who is the coat-room boy, evidently tried to steal the clasp. When I confronted him just now and threatened to call the police, he gave it up.

EDDIE. That's a lie! I found the pin on the floor. I was going to turn it in after the show!

SYLVIA. The pin may have dropped on the floor.

SEAVER. You sure this is your pin?

SYLVIA. [*Without even looking.*] Yes, I am.

CARL. [*A little heatedly.*] Certainly she's sure!

SEAVER. [*First looking at* SYLVIA, *and then at* CARL.] Who are you?

CARL. [*Preposterous question.*] I'm this lady's husband! [SYLVIA *looks at him. From Right,* JOE *and* HEALY *are coming down.* HEALY *is another detective.* SEAVER *sees them immediately, puts aside the pin nonsense at once and goes toward* JOE.]

SEAVER. This is going to be great. Just great!

JOE. I'm sorry, Captain.

SEAVER. A guy breaks out of a theatre! What are the papers going to say? [*Louder.*] What's the commissioner going to say? What the hell was he DOING in a theatre?

JOE. I'm sorry. You knew he was here. I phoned you. I didn't think you wanted me to take him back to the Tombs.

SEAVER. What the hell did you have to miss the train for?

JOE. I'm sorry.

SEAVER. [*To* HEALY.] What's been done?

HEALY. We've got men posted at the subway and elevated. We've got the block surrounded and men going through every building. We've called all the patrol cars in this district and we're covering Pennsylvania station and the Grand Central.

SEAVER. A lot of good that'll do in Times Square.

JOE. He must be on the block some place. He can't get off it. [*There is the sound of applause from above.*]

MAC. They'll be coming down in a minute. Captain, if there's any scandal, I'll get blamed.

SEAVER. [*To* JOE, *indicating with his head.*] Show me how he got out.

MAC. Please, Captain. [JOE *starts toward Men's,* HEALY *following.*]

SEAVER. Keep your shirt on.

CARL. May I please have my pin?

SEAVER. I'll find out whose it is later. I got my own troubles here. Just stick around.

CARL. I don't understand, officer. Don't you believe it's mine?

SEAVER. Mister, I'm not in the believing business. If it's yours you'll stick around. [*To* EDDIE.] Don't you leave the theatre.

EDDIE. No, sir. [SEAVER *strides into Men's followed by* JOE *and* HEALY. *The* TWELVE YEAR OLD GIRL *runs down from Right and into Ladies'.*]

MAC. Did you take it, Eddie?

EDDIE. No, Mac.

KITTY. [*Coming down Left followed by* ANNA *and* MAE.] He's a salesman at Macy's.

ANNA. That's not what he told me.

MAE. Shut up, the both of you. [KITTY *and* ANNA *go into the Ladies' room.* SYLVIA *starts to exit, Left.* CARL *feels it necessary to say something to maintain their relationship in the eyes of the others.*]

CARL. I'll meet you here later, dear.

SYLVIA. [*Looks at him, simply.*] Yes. [*And exits, Left.*]

MAC. [*To* EDDIE.] Better help with the coffee. [CARL *goes to the water fountain. The* USHERS *come out of Ladies' and go to the coffee table. From Right* ANDERSON *comes down, and halfway down the stairs—calls to* MAE.]

ANDERSON. "Psst." [HE *attracts her attention.* MAE *starts on seeing him, and goes fearfully, looking back.*]

ANDERSON. [*Quietly.*] Did you get the money?

MAE. [*Tensely.*] What are you doing here?

ANDERSON. I thought you wanted me to come.

MAE. Go away! Beat it! [ANDERSON *stands there, puzzled.*] Go away! Get the hell out of here! [ANDERSON *turns and goes slowly upstairs, Right, mystified.* SEAVER, JOE *and* HEALY *come out of Men's room and head toward stairs, Right.*]

JOE. I shot while he was still in the window. I don't see how he got out of the alley that quick.

SEAVER. He could've climbed on that roof. [*To* HEALY.] You go on the roof.

JOE. [*Stopping four steps up.*] I been up there.

SEAVER. Look around anyway.

HEALY. Yes, sir. [*Exits up stairs.*]

JOE. Why don't you come up and see for yourself?

SEAVER. Don't worry, I will. Wait a minute. I've got to phone first. [SEAVER *starts for phone booth and reaches it before he spies the "Out of Order" sign. He stops.*]

JOE. That one there is working. [SEAVER *turns and goes toward it. By now both staircases are crowded with audience entering lounge.*]

STANLEY. [*Halfway downstairs, Right.*] There he is. You look just the same!

GEORGE. [*Entering Left and meeting* STANLEY *center of stage.*] So do you, kid!

[*They shake hands vigorously.* SEAVER *inserts coin in the wall phone and the chatter increases as the Curtain comes down slowly.*]

ACT THREE

ACT THREE

The curtain rises on the same scene ten minutes later. Positions have altered a little. Someone is going upstairs, someone down. The coffee drinking is in its last stages, the USHERS *are mostly gathering things.*

MA. How are you going to sleep tonight? That's your third cup.

HERMAN. I almost fell asleep upstairs. I couldn't hear a word they were saying.

GEORGE. It was the first time we ever smoked a cigar! And then we all went back to the frat house and dragged them out of bed just as they were!

JOHNSON. [*Speaking anxiously to* CARL, *who isn't especially interested and who is seated on couch.*] I don't know whether to be more worried or not. I read that a Cæsarian operation is even safer than a normal delivery—but—an operation! I don't know what to think—

MA. I won't go to another show next year.

HERMAN. Last year we heard fine. You just got to be lucky and pick out loud actors.

MA. Why didn't you make the man show you where the seats were? That's what I'd do.

75

HERMAN. I saw some empty seats up front. We ought to sit in them.

MA. I won't do it.

HERMAN. How're they going to know it? They only look at your tickets when you come in. [LITTLE GIRL *runs out of the Ladies' room and exits, Right.*]

GEORGE. [*Going great.*] . . . There we were—fifty students on the campus—and all of us stark naked!

STANLEY. [*Just as excited.*] We didn't even have time to get towels!

GEORGE. The newspapers kept writing about it for months. They couldn't see how a swimming pool could catch fire! [*The three men laugh.*] I don't see how either! [SEAVER, JOE *and* HEALY *come down the stairs, Right. They will enter Men's.*]

SEAVER. If we don't pick that wop up tonight we'll be in a great spot. With Colorado calling us up.

TAFT. We'll get him.

HEALY. I think I'll try some of that coffee. It looks pretty good. [*The* BUZZER *sounds and there is the surge to both staircases.*]

EDDIE. Curtain going up! Curtain going up!

MA. Are you going to do it?

HERMAN. [*Following her.*] Certainly. The seats are empty anyway.

MA. They'll make us pay extra.

HERMAN. [*Placing cup at foot of stairs and exiting, Right.*] I'd like to see them try it.

STANLEY. George, I can't tell you what a big kick I got out of seeing you.

GEORGE. Stanley, I feel like a college kid again.

JOHNSON. [*Following* CARL.] I'd go to my wife and be with her through the operation but I'm afraid I'd make the doctor nervous.

CARL. Yes, you'd better stay here. [*Walking up the stairs.*]

JOHNSON. How long do you think a Cæsarian operation takes?

CARL. I don't know. I've never had one. [*They both exit.*]

GEORGE. I'm awfully glad to have met you, Donald.

DONALD. Same here, George.

STANLEY. We'll get together regularly from now on, and I mean that. You know where to get me.

GEORGE. Sure thing.

MRS. MADISON. Good-bye. I'll be expecting to see you soon.

GEORGE. You'll see me sooner than you expect, Mrs. Madison. And let me tell you something. You're just what I knew Stanley's mother would be like! [*There is a terrible moment of stiffening.* MRS. MADISON *draws her hand away as from a leper.* STANLEY *takes her under the arm and wheels her right about face.*]

STANLEY. [*Loftily.*] Come on, Lilly! [*They start to march Right.* GEORGE *stands there, flabbergasted.* DONALD *takes a quick step toward* GEORGE, *grabs his hand*

*and pumps it in gratitude. He gestures with his hand
"Thank you, brother" and turns to run after his
brother.* GEORGE *slowly walks Right, out, shaking his
head. All have either straggled or hastened out both
exits. The three* USHERS *have gathered up all the coffee
implements on the trays.*]

MAC. You girls take the coffee things back, Eddie has
to stay down here.

MAE. Yes, sir. [*They hurry, and start out, looking
oddly at* EDDIE *and the three strange, important men.*]
MAC. [*To* SEAVER *who comes out of Men's room with*
JOE *and* HEALY.] Would you like some coffee before
they go?

SEAVER. No.

MAC. Go 'head, girls. [*All are out now, except for* ED-
DIE, JOE, SEAVER, HEALY *and* MAC. *They all look to*
SEAVER.]

SEAVER. Healy. Find out if they've picked him up yet.
[HEALY *goes to phone on wall, inserts coin and dials.*]

SEAVER. Do you want to know something? You cost me
a hundred bucks.

JOE. How do you mean?

SEAVER. That gas station in Colorado offered a hundred
bucks reward for Mako—dead or alive—and it was
coming to me.

JOE. You'll get it.

SEAVER. How? Whoever picks him up this time'll want
it. Damn it, how did he get that gun?

JOE. I told you, Seaver. He lifted it from the ticket man.

SEAVER. While he was handcuffed to you? I don't believe it. No pick-pocket's that good. Listen, you didn't have the cuffs on him.

JOE. The hell I didn't!

HEALY. [*At phone.*] This is Healy. Has Mako been picked up? [*He turns toward* SEAVER, *the phone still to his ear, listening, and shakes his head negatively.*] One minute. [*To* SEAVER.] Corrigan says Madison Square Garden'll be out in half an hour and he thinks you ought to call the traffic squad back.

SEAVER. They stay out! And if he's not found by one o'clock they're to stay on duty and the next shift joins 'em!

HEALY. Yes, sir. [*Into phone.*] Corrigan, Captain Seaver says to keep them out and not to relieve them at one o'clock. The next shift is to join 'em. Right. [*He hangs up and looks to* SEAVER, *who looks to* JOE.]

SEAVER. You got your ticket stubs?

JOE. [*Taking them out of his coat pocket.*] Yes.

SEAVER. [*To* HEALY.] Healy, go upstairs and see who's sitting on either side of those seats.

HEALY. Yes, sir.

JOE. We were sitting on the aisle.

SEAVER. Did you see who was sitting in the third seat?

JOE. No. I didn't notice.

SEAVER. [*To* HEALY.] Take a look anyway.

MAC. [*To* HEALY.] Please don't make any commotion. [*To* SEAVER.] I'll lose my job if there's any trouble.

SEAVER. [*To* HEALY.] Be quiet.

HEALY. Yes, sir, [*Exits.* SEAVER *thinks a moment.*]

SEAVER. I still don't see how the hell he got that gun?

JOE. [*Evenly.*] He lifted it, Seaver, while we were smoking upstairs.

SEAVER. While he was handcuffed to you he was able to take a revolver out of somebody's pocket!

JOE. He did.

MAC. [*Defensively.*] It wasn't my fault. I didn't feel anything.

SEAVER. Show me how he did it! Act it out. Where were you standing?

TAFT. It was in the lobby upstairs. We went out for a smoke. And— [*He has* MAC *by the elbow, he motions to* EDDIE.] Come here. [EDDIE *comes to him, and he places him in position as he talks.*] We were all pretty close together. [*He illustrates.*] I kept my coat over my arm to hide the handcuffs. Then he asked for a cigarette—and I gave it to him. [*He starts to put his left hand in his pocket.*]

SEAVER. Say! [JOE *stops his hand.*] How come he had his right hand free? The cuffs are supposed to be on his right hand and your left. You know that.

JOE. [*Resenting the implication.*] I'm left-handed.

SEAVER. [*Nodding slightly in irritation.*] Go 'head. He asked for a cigarette.

JOE. I had the cigarettes in my pocket, and I gave him one. He took it— [*He takes the cigarette case out of his left pocket and shows how he did it, the case opening as he presses the catch.* SEAVER'S *gaze is riveted on what he sees, and so is* JOE'S *since the folded money is exposed.* SEAVER *looks up at* JOE, *who hasn't recovered yet.* JOE *looks squarely at him.* SEAVER *takes the money from the case, still looking at* JOE *for a reaction. He starts to count it and hands it back.* JOE *speaks first, calmly.*]

JOE. Well, what of it?

SEAVER. Five hundred bucks, Taft.

JOE. I'm allowed to carry it in a cigarette case.

SEAVER. You never had five hundred bucks at once in your life.

JOE. [*Even steadier than* SEAVER.] I been carrying it for weeks.

SEAVER. Taft, something stinks around here!

JOE. What are you trying to say, Seaver?

SEAVER. That gun! Someone handed it to him!

JOE. [*Louder.*] And I tell you he lifted it!

SEAVER. [*Still louder.*] And I tell you I don't believe you! [*Quietly.*] Let's see your gun. [JOE, *grim, takes his gun out of his back pocket and shows it to him.* SEAVER *breaks it, looks at the contents and then returns it. He thinks for a moment, then steps to* MAC *and grabs him suddenly by his coat lapel.*] Listen you, you gave him that gun! I know you did!

MAC. [*Frightened into blubbering.*] I didn't . . . no
. . . no . . . honest to God . . . I didn't. [*His child-
ish fright makes it immediately evident that the stab in
the dark is fruitless.* SEAVER *releases him and relaxes in
disgust.*]

SEAVER. [*Kindly.*] Pull yourself together!

MAC. Yes, sir. [SEAVER *looks at* JOE, *who returns his
look, expressionless. From Right comes* HEALY, *prod-
ding* MA *and* HERMAN *before him. They all look to the
group.*]

HEALY. [*From top of stairs.*] Captain, these people
were IN the seats! [SEAVER *walks slowly toward them,
sizing them up. Right off he doesn't think these people
can be very guilty of anything.*]

HERMAN. [*A hair-breadth from nervous apoplexy.*]
We didn't think anybody'd mind—

MA. The seats were empty anyway. [SEAVER *is still
looking at them.* MAC, *ever conscientious, steps forward
to soothe his customers.*]

MAC. It's all right, this man's a detective. [MA *and* HER-
MAN *react sharply.*]

HERMAN. [*Whimpering.*] We didn't mean any harm—
we couldn't hear from the back—

MA. We were only sitting there a minute—

SEAVER. All right, go back to your seats.

HERMAN. [*Gratefully, retreating.*] Yes, sir. Thank you,
thank you.

MA. We'll sit in the back—we can hear fine— [SEAVER

looks at HEALY, *not admiringly, as the couple go up-stairs.*] I told you we'd get caught!

HERMAN. Imagine hiring detectives! [*And they are out.*]

SEAVER. Who was sitting in that third seat?

HEALY. A girl about twelve years old.

SEAVER. A girl twelve years old. That's fine. That's just dandy! Let's get the hell out of here! [HEALY *starts Left with* SEAVER.] Taft, you stay here. [*To* EDDIE.] Tell those people I took the pin to the Forty-Seventh Street Station and they can get it after the show. You come up, too.

EDDIE. Yes, sir. [*From Right* ANDERSON *has come partly downstairs, stopped and turned to go back quickly.* ANDERSON *evidently saw* HEALY *or* SEAVER *and decided to leave.* HEALY, *however, has seen him and is galvanized into action.*]

HEALY. Hey! [*He starts to run up the stairs.* ANDERSON *slips on the stairs and sprawls.*] Come back here! [HEALY *gets to him halfway up the stairs and brings him down.*]

SEAVER. ANDERSON!!!

ANDERSON. What's the matter?

SEAVER. [*Coming quickly toward him.*] I knew it! I knew somebody was mixed up in this!

ANDERSON. [*Coming down.*] I haven't done anything.

SEAVER. [*Taking him by the lapel.*] Anderson, where is he? WHERE IS HE?

ANDERSON. Where's who? [*He looks around.*] What is this? A frame-up?

SEAVER. Don't start playing dumb, Anderson, I'll murder you! Where's Mako?

ANDERSON. Mako? I don't know.

SEAVER. Don't start that, I'll brain you! [*He shakes him and throws him on centre couch.*] Out with it! Where is he?

ANDERSON. He's been caught—he's in jail. Or he's on his way to Colorado to get hung.

SEAVER. You know damn well he got away!

ANDERSON. No! Oh! I didn't know it!

SEAVER. [*To* JOE, *looking at his watch.*] The theatre crowd'll be out in twenty minutes. [*To* ANDERSON.] I'm taking you to the office. Anderson, I'm going to kick hell out of you. I'll give you the worst licking you've ever had, you'll spend the next six months in a hospital. Are you going to tell me where Mako is?

ANDERSON. [*Frantic, pleading.*] I don't know. Honest to God, I wouldn't help him. He hates my guts, he only came back to New York to get me. I've been under cover. Ask Taft.

JOE. He's no friend of Mako's. What *are* you doing here?

ANDERSON. My wife called me. She told me to come here.

SEAVER. Your wife?

ANDERSON. She works here, she's an usher. I just got her message half an hour ago and I came right over.

SEAVER. What's her name?

ANDERSON. Mae. Mae Danish. [SEAVER *looks at* MAC.]

MAC. Yes. She works here.

EDDIE. Oh! [*The exclamation has escaped him involuntarily. He starts to run upstairs.*]

SEAVER. [*A shout.*] Hey! [*This alone stops* EDDIE.] Where are you going?

EDDIE. [*Top of stairs.*] No place.

SEAVER. Come down here. [*He walks to* EDDIE *and eyes him.*] What the hell do you know about this?

EDDIE. Nothing. I don't know anything about it.

SEAVER. Well, you just stick around. [*He turns and looks around. He thinks and comes to a reluctant decision.*] I might as well take it on the chin now as later. [*To* HEALY.] Call the commissioner at his house.

HEALY. Yes, sir.

SEAVER. [*Looking ahead, dully.*] Rhinelander 7-6300. If he wants to come down we'll be at the office. [HEALY *goes to the wall phone as* SYLVIA *and* CARL *enter, Left.* SEAVER *watches* CARL *advance to him.* HEALY *dials, and will hang up, insert the coin again and listen a second time to make sure there is no answer.*]

CARL. My wife and I have discussed this, officer, and we've decided we'd rather not press charges.

SEAVER. Press what charges?

CARL. Against this boy. I may have been a bit hasty in accusing him, I really haven't proof he didn't find the pin on the floor, as he says.

SYLVIA. I've lost it before. The catch isn't very good. [SEAVER *looks at* EDDIE, *thinking.*]

EDDIE. I found it on the floor. I wasn't keeping it.

SEAVER. [*Taking the pin from his pocket and looking at it.*] Do you think it's this lady's pin?

EDDIE. Yes, sir. I think so.

SEAVER. But you're not sure?

EDDIE. [*Wanting* SYLVIA *to get the pin back, but nervous of stepping into something.*] I'm pretty sure. Yes, I'm positive.

SEAVER. If you found it on the floor how can you be sure it's hers?

EDDIE. [*Trapped, fumbling his way out.*] She says it's hers. I'm not really sure.

CARL. Frankly, officer, I don't understand your attitude. Surely we don't look like thieves and if we tell you it's our pin, and this boy admits it's our pin, why do you insist on a regular investigation?

SEAVER. This is pretty expensive, mister, and I don't want to hand it over on my responsibility. Is it insured?

CARL. Did you insure it, dear?

SYLVIA. Yes, it's insured. [HEALY *hangs up, and* SEAVER *looks toward him.*]

HEALY. No one answers.

SEAVER. All right, let it go. Well, you leave it with me. Tomorrow I'll send someone over to your office and he can check this with your insurance company. That's all right, isn't it?

CARL. [*Carrying it off great, but probably nervous.*] It certainly is not! Why should I be subjected to the embarrassment of a policeman in my office? I'm demanding my property. If you feel you still want to withhold it, you may—and I assure you that you'll regret the consequences. [*From Left,* FRANK *has come down unnoticed, and has gone to* SYLVIA.]

FRANK. Mrs. Temple. [SYLVIA *turns and looks at him, expressionless.*] Mister Temple's here in his car. He said he'd drive around until the show was over and he'd take you home.

SYLVIA. All right, Frank.

FRANK. He dismissed me for the evening. Shall I continue looking for the pin?

CARL. No, we've found it. You can go now. [FRANK *looks at him, surprised to get an order, but recovers in an instant.*]

SYLVIA. [*Still trying to cover up.*] I'll call you in the morning, Frank. Goodnight.

FRANK. Yes, ma'm. Goodnight, Mrs. Temple. [*He bows, turns, running up the stairs Left.*]

CARL. [*Calling after* FRANK, *to look natural.*] Good night. [FRANK *turns and looks at* CARL *surprised. He exits.*]

EDDIE. The only reason I thought it could be this lady's

pin is because it was right under her coat. It was a fur coat—and I remember hanging it up by itself not to get creased—

SEAVER. [*Who has been puzzled, not paying* EDDIE *any attention, but looking after* FRANK.] You're Mrs. Temple?

SYLVIA. Yes.

SEAVER. And who did you say you were?

CARL. I've told you I'm Mister Temple. [*He tries a small laugh.*] The Mister Temple my chauffeur mentioned is my father.

SYLVIA. [*Smilingly.*] Yes, I'm afraid I only have one husband.

SEAVER. [*After a look from one to the other. To* JOE.] Get ahold of that chauffeur. [JOE *exits, Left.* MAC *has spied something on the carpet near the telephone, and is bending over.*]

CARL. [*Good and indignant.*] I certainly resent this! You haven't the right to do what you're doing and you know it! You keep the pin until tomorrow morning and I'll straighten this out with the proper authorities.

MAC. Say! [*They* ALL *look toward him.*] Here's blood! Look at this! It's blood! [SEAVER *walks right over, bends down, touches his finger to it and looks.* MAC *has spied more of it under the dial telephone.*] Here's a lot of it.

SEAVER. Where did he get shot—in here?

MAC. [*Pointing.*] No. Mister Taft shot at him in there as he was going through the window.

CARL. [*Having taken* SYLVIA *by the arm.*] Come dear, there's no use our staying and—

SEAVER. [*A shout at them.*] Stay here! [*Back to* MAC.] Didn't he run in here?

MAC. No, I was in here. He jumped out the window.

SEAVER. He got back here! He telephoned somebody! [*He thinks furiously, tense. From* ANDERSON *there is a guttural sound as the realization comes to him.* SEAVER *whirls to look at him.*]

ANDERSON. He called me! He told me to come here!

SEAVER. I thought you said your wife called you!

ANDERSON. No, he called me! I didn't recognize his voice! He said he had a message from my wife!

SEAVER. He's hanging around here!

ANDERSON. [*Frantic.*] What'd I tell you! He's waiting for me some place! He'll kill me!

SEAVER. [*Looking at the carpet again, and starting slowly to follow the blood trail.*] Now where the hell does this lead to?

ANDERSON. [*Throwing himself on* SEAVER.] You got to protect me! [*The music starts above and some blond, romantic juvenile will sing his piffling love song through the worst of it.*]

ANDERSON. Take me to jail! I'll go any place! [SEAVER *disengages him and starts to follow the floor marks.*] He'll get me—he's crazy, I tell you—and he's a killer— I know him— [*His last phrase ends in a shriek. The phone booth flies open abruptly.* MAKO *is out in a step.*

His left hand is now entirely covered with blood, wet.
His arm hangs limp. In his right hand he has his gun,
held easily and expertly. He seems wound-up, cat-like.
His first words are clipped, arresting.]

MAKO. Stand where you are. [*Everyone freezes still.*
SEAVER *moves almost imperceptibly for his gun.* SYLVIA,
her hand to her mouth, gasps a frightened "Oh!".] Put
your hands up! [*All the men do,* SEAVER *slowly,* ANDER-
SON *fearfully, rigid with terror.*] Up!

SEAVER. Don't be a fool, Mako. You can't get off this
block.

MAKO. You don't see me trying. [*He has been looking*
hungrily at ANDERSON *all the time.*] How do you feel,
Anderson? Squealing again. You always did talk too
much.

ANDERSON. Tony, for God's sake, I didn't squeal on
you! They knew it anyway. They came to me first.
Honest to God they did!

MAKO. [*As though he never even heard him.*] I could
shoot you in the head—but I wouldn't do it. You'd be
dead too quick.

SEAVER. Mako—don't do it! I'll try to help you! I'll get
you life imprisonment! You can trust me, Mako!

MAKO. [*Unheeding.*] But I want you to die slow. I
want you to die in pain—with a bullet in your stom-
ach—

ANDERSON. Tony!

MAKO. That's the worst place. Your insides'll be on fire
—you'll feel like your guts are burning—it's worse than

hanging—Anderson— [*With an agonized cry from* ANDERSON, MAKO *fires, once, confidently. With a moan* ANDERSON, *shot, sinks to the floor, conscious.* MAKO *has turned his gun on* SEAVER, *who has wrenched forward at the shot.*]

TONY. [*A bark.*] Don't move! [SYLVIA, *horrified, goes close to* CARL, *her face in her hands.*] How is it, Anderson? Don't be dead too quick. You'd like another bullet, my friend, but you can't have it. They wouldn't kill me quick either. They were going to hang me. [ANDERSON *is still.*] Already, eh? Don't try anything. [*To everyone.*] I only get hung once. Anybody I kill now is on the house. [*He starts to back out, Right.*] Don't start after me—stay where you are. [*He walks upstairs very slow.*] You'll only save yourself from getting hurt —I don't want to shoot anybody— [*From the Right staircase comes* JOE, *his gun already in his hand, moving quietly on the carpeted floor.* MAKO *stops short and stands stock still for a moment. The people before him are staring at something behind. The realization of danger comes and he whirls, but before he can shoot,* JOE *does, twice, quickly.* MAKO *crumples, the gun dropping from his limp hand and landing even before he does.* MAC, EDDIE *and* CARL *are horrified, putting their hands down, but looking dazedly on.* SYLVIA, *white, just this side of hysteria, sobs in her hands.* SEAVER, *from the instant of* JOE'S *shots, rushes to* MAKO. HEALY *goes to* ANDERSON. JOE *comes quickly to* MAKO, *too, and they both bend over him.*]

SEAVER. He's alive. [*He lifts* MAKO'S *head up.* MAKO *opens his eyes, turns his head to look at* JOE *and mumbles something in Italian and then falls back.*] Not now he isn't.

JOE. He said something in Italian.

SEAVER. Yeh. Well, let's get the both of 'em out of here. Take 'em to the morgue.

HEALY. [*Starting to the dial phone.*] Should I call the wagon?

SEAVER. Yeah. No! It'll only tie up the theatre traffic. Take 'em in a cab.

CARL. [*Who has been consoling* SYLVIA, *one eye, however, on* SEAVER.] Control yourself, dear.

HEALY. [*To* EDDIE.] Give me a hand, kid.

EDDIE. Me? [EDDIE *goes over to* HEALY. HEALY *takes the head,* EDDIE *the legs of* ANDERSON *and they exit, Left, while the scene is progressing.* JOE *starts to lift* MAKO, *taking him under the shoulders.*]

JOE. Come on, Mac. [MAC *takes* MAKO'S *legs.*]

MAC. I hope nobody sees us. A thing like this can give the theatre a bad name. [SEAVER *goes to the dial phone, drops a coin and dials.*]

CARL. [SYLVIA *has her handkerchief to her face.*] Pull yourself together, dear. [CARL *walks to* SEAVER *to talk to him, standing behind him while he phones.*]

SEAVER. [*Into phone.*] Corrigan? This is Seaver! I got Mako! [*He laughs.*] Call the traffic squad back. [*Cheerily.*] Lucky? I'll say so! Say Corrigan, have you made out the commissioner's report yet? Uh huh. Well, we don't have to put it exactly that way. He didn't really escape, he was shot resisting arrest. Yeah. Uh huh. I'll be up in fifteen minutes. [*He hangs up and beams at* CARL.]

CARL. My wife is rather upset, as you can imagine. If I could please have the pin I'd like to take her home.

SEAVER. [*Taking the pin from his pocket immediately, but holding it in his right hand as he points and talks.*] Listen, Mister Temple, I want you to get this right. I wasn't trying to be tough or anything, but my job's like everybody else's—you can't make too many mistakes.

CARL. I understand that.

SEAVER. I was just doing what I had to, and with all that going on, you know— [*There is a sobbing from upstairs, Left. He starts toward the steps.* KITTY *and* EDDIE, *supporting* MAE *between them, come down.* MAE *is blank-faced, dazed.*]

EDDIE. [*To* SEAVER.] She fainted. [KITTY *takes her into Ladies'.*]

SEAVER. [*To* EDDIE.] This pin belongs to the lady, doesn't it?

EDDIE. [*Still apprehensive.*] I think so.

SEAVER. [*Pleasantly, winningly.*] Come on, son. You're not being arrested. It was on the lady's coat.

EDDIE. I didn't take it from her coat!

SEAVER. [*Impatiently, turning to* CARL *and* SYLVIA, *who has gotten up.*] Well, I think it's yours, Mrs. Temple. [*He hands it to her.*] I'm sorry you've been put out like this—

SYLVIA. It's all right, it wasn't your fault.

SEAVER. Thank you ma'm. And I'll tell you what I'll do about the pin. It'll save us all trouble. [*To* CARL.] I'll drop over to your office, Mister Temple, tomorrow, myself, and we'll call up the insurance company and identify it. [*He smiles, having done them this magnificent favor.*] That's all right, isn't it?

CARL. [*Stuck for once, while* SYLVIA *looks horrified at him.*] Why, yes, I guess that'll be all right.

SEAVER. [*Putting out his hand, which* CARL *takes.*] Goodnight Mrs. Temple. Goodnight, Mister Temple —I'll see you sometime tomorrow. [*He starts to exit Left.*]

CARL. Goodnight.

SYLVIA. Just a minute. This isn't my pin.

SEAVER. What?

SYLVIA. This is not my pin.

SEAVER. It isn't?

SYLVIA. I'm sure it isn't. Mine was a different shape, and had a pendant—it isn't like this at all. [*To* CARL.] You know it. [CARL *looks.*]

CARL. [*Rising to it.*] Why, how stupid of me. I'm terribly sorry, sir. All this trouble we've made— [JOE *has come down Right and he has* SEAVER'S *attention.* SYLVIA *hands the pin to* SEAVER.]

SEAVER. Well!

SYLVIA. [*To* SEAVER.] I must have lost it in the car. I remember now. I kept fixing it to my collar—

SEAVER. [*To* JOE.] You get 'em out all right?

JOE. Yeah.

SEAVER. [*Impatiently.*] Yes! That's where it must be, lady.

CARL. I hope you'll excuse us.

SEAVER. That's all right. [*To* EDDIE, *who has been an amazed listener.*] The owner of this'll show up screaming tonight or tomorrow. Send her to the Forty-Seventh Street Station. The pin'll be in the Lost and Found Department.

EDDIE. Yes, sir. [SYLVIA *exits Left,* CARL *following.*]

SEAVER. [*Crossing to* JOE, *putting the pin in his pocket.*] Say, Joe. That hundred dollars for the wop— I think I'm entitled to half of it.

JOE. No, it's yours. You can have it all.

SEAVER. Oh, hell, no. You're entitled to half of it.

EDDIE. [*Who has been looking at* SEAVER.] What happens to the pin if nobody comes for it?

SEAVER. [*A little harshly.*] You mean who gets it?

EDDIE. Yes.

SEAVER. You do. In six months. [*His tone ridicules* EDDIE'S *preposterous hope that so valuable a pin won't be called for.*] But don't count on it! [EDDIE'S *stare is lost on him as he turns back to* JOE *immediately.*] Now listen, we'll go half on it, Joe.

JOE. It's all yours. I won't touch it.

SEAVER. Say, that's damned sweet of you. I need it too. [*He puts his arm through his and they start to the Men's.*] I want to apologize, Joe, for flying off the handle like that. You know how it is— [*And they have exited into Men's.* KITTY *has come out of Ladies'.*]

KITTY. Gee whiz, Mae was like deleerious. She kept laughing and saying it was a big joke—her baby's got no father! You know what I think?

EDDIE. What?

KITTY. Mae's gonna have a baby! [*The overture starts from above.* KITTY *looks up.*] Say! [*She runs off Left.* HELEN *comes down Right and* EDDIE *sees her. He goes to her quickly.*]

EDDIE. Helen! You don't know what's happened. Mae was married. She was married! She was only trying to get money out of me!

HELEN. [*In a strange voice.*] You mean—you don't have to have two hundred dollars?

EDDIE. No! And what I nearly did to get it! All the trouble we could've had! But everything is all right now. [*From Right, the top of the stairs,* MAC *appears.*]

MAC. Eddie! Hurry up! [*He disappears.*]

EDDIE. Darling! I'll tell you about it later. There's so many things! And you're going to get a diamond pin! Honest! [*He turns and runs up the remaining half flight of stairs, stopping at the top.*] Isn't everything wonderful! [*He exits.* HELEN, *her face expressionless, walks as though in a trance to the centre couch, and sits. The* TWO GIRLS *have come down Left, their hats in their hands, to be put on in Ladies'.*]

FIRST GIRL. I didn't hear that part. I turned around and I saw they were carrying two drunken men outside—

and by that time— [*Both are in Ladies'. The* LITTLE GIRL *runs to Ladies' room from Right.* DONALD MADISON *has come down Left, and entered Men's.* JOHNSON *has come down Left, gone to the dial phone, and dialed.*]

JOHNSON. Fourth floor, please. [GEORGE NELSON *comes down Right and crosses to Men's. Into phone.*] Can I speak to Mister Neil? Sam—what? [*He stops short.*] A boy! No! Yeah, sure that's what I wanted. She wants to see me? I'll be right up! [MAE *comes out of Ladies', now composed. She picks up a stack of programs which are on the coffee table.* JOHNSON *hangs up and turns around with a joyous face.*] Say, I just got a son! [MAE *looks at him, no emotion.*] A boy! You're the first one who knows it! While the show was going on! [MAE *is listless.*] Give me a program! [SHE *does,* HE *grabs at it.*] I'm going to frame this! I'll show it to him when he grows up! [*He has been looking at it oddly while going up stairs Left.*] My gosh! Say! I've seen this show before! [*He exits, hurriedly Left.* CARL, *comes down Right and crosses to* MAE. CARL *looks at* MAE, *who looks back. The* TWO GIRLS *exit from Ladies'. The* FIRST GIRL *sees* MAE.]

FIRST GIRL. Remember when the adagio dancer fell and the woman screamed from the back? [*The* SECOND GIRL *nods.*] That usher did it. I turned around.

SECOND GIRL. [*Both are exiting Right.*] No?

FIRST GIRL. Sure, she does it every performance. They want you to think it's somebody in the audience getting excited. [*They have exited.* LITTLE GIRL *runs from the Ladies' and exits Right.*]

CARL. [*Quietly.*] May I see you this Sunday?

MAE. What'll your wife say?

CARL. My wife!

MAE. Wasn't that your wife you were talking to?

CARL. [*Amused.*] Why, no. She's just an acquaintance I happened to run into.

MAE. [*As though thinking it over. A coquettish smile.*] I don't know. Do you want to?

CARL. I'd like to very much.

MAE. [*Archly.*] You're not a married man, are you?

CARL. [*Amused, shaking his head.*] No.

MAE. Why wait until Sunday?

CARL. You're sweet. Pick you up on Sixth Avenue corner in fifteen minutes.

MAE. All rightie. [*He smiles again, turns and exits Left.* MAE's *smile disappears. She starts to cross Left to exit.* HELEN *has not heard anything. Her head is back, resting on the couch. Her face is still expressionless.*]

NELSON. [*Exiting from Men's with* DONALD MADISON.] How could he marry an old dame like that?

DONALD. I almost dropped dead when I saw her! This has been some visit for me!

NELSON. Why don't we both go out by ourselves tonight and get drunk?

DONALD. Boy, you're talking to a friend! [*They are out,*

Left. SEAVER *and* JOE *come out of Men's, arm in arm. They will cross to Right.*]

SEAVER. Do you know what Mako said just before he passed out?

TAFT. You mean in Italian?

SEAVER. Yeah. He looked at you and said, "My good friend, I thank you." [JOE *looks at him.*] I guess your mind goes just before you kick off. [*Both exit Right.* MAC *comes down Left, carrying the ticket-stub-box, and as he is at the foot of stairs, the telephone in the booth starts ringing. The same steady ring. He puts the box down.* MAC *starts to count, walking toward the phone booth.*]

MAC. One—two—three—four—five—six—seven—eight—nine—ten. [*He has opened the booth. He takes the receiver off the hook.*] Hello? [*He puts the receiver back. He pulls the cord and the booth lights up. He closes the door. He takes off the "Out of Order" sign, and smiles at* HELEN.] That's funny. Did you enjoy the show, Miss? [*He picks up the box and exits into Men's.* HELEN *slowly lifts her head. She looks down at her purse. For a second she stares at it dully, and then, as though it is distasteful, pushes it from her. It falls to the floor. She quickly drops her face into her hands, sobbing, as the exit music swells, happily, tum, ta, ta, ta, as*

THE CURTAIN COMES SLOWLY DOWN